Protecting
Ideas

Protecting
Ideas

David L. Hudson, Jr.

SERIES CONSULTING EDITOR
Alan Marzilli, M.A., J.D.

CHELSEA HOUSE
PUBLISHERS
A Haights Cross Communications Company ®

Philadelphia

CHELSEA HOUSE PUBLISHERS

VP, New Product Development Sally Cheney
Director of Production Kim Shinners
Creative Manager Takeshi Takahashi
Manufacturing Manager Diann Grasse

Staff for PROTECTING IDEAS

Executive Editor Lee Marcott
Editorial Assistant Carla Greenberg
Photo Editor Sarah Bloom
Production Editor Bonnie Cohen
Series and Cover Designer Keith Trego
Layout 21st Century Publishing and Communications, Inc.

A Haights Cross Communications ✦ Company ®

http://www.chelseahouse.com

First Printing

1 3 5 7 9 8 6 4 2

Library of Congress Cataloging-in-Publication Data

Hudson, David L., 1969–
    Protecting ideas/David L. Hudson
        p. cm.—(Point/counterpoint)
    Includes bibliographical references and index.
    ISBN 0-7910-8646-1 (hard cover)
    1. Intellectual property—United States. I. Title. II. Point/counterpoint
(Philadelphia, Pa.)
KF2980.H83 2005
3346.7304'8—dc22

                                                                2005013295

All links and web addresses were checked and verified to be correct at the time of
publication. Because of the dynamic nature of the web, some addresses and links
may have changed since publication and may no longer be valid.

||||||||CONTENTS

Foreword

Alan Marzilli, M.A., J.D.
Durham, North Carolina

The debates presented in POINT/COUNTERPOINT are among the most interesting and controversial in contemporary American society, but studying them is more than an academic activity. They affect every citizen; they are the issues that today's leaders debate and tomorrow's will decide. The reader may one day play a central role in resolving them.

Why study both sides of the debate? It's possible that the reader will not yet have formed any opinion at all on the subject of this volume—but this is unlikely. It is more likely that the reader will already hold an opinion, probably a strong one, and very probably one formed without full exposure to the arguments of the other side. It is rare to hear an argument presented in a balanced way, and it is easy to form an opinion on too little information; these books will help to fill in the informational gaps that can never be avoided. More important, though, is the practical function of the series: Skillful argumentation requires a thorough knowledge of *both* sides—though there are seldom only two, and only by knowing what an opponent is likely to assert can one form an articulate response.

Perhaps more important is that listening to the other side sometimes helps one to see an opponent's arguments in a more human way. For example, Sister Helen Prejean, one of the nation's most visible opponents of capital punishment, has been deeply affected by her interactions with the families of murder victims. Seeing the families' grief and pain, she understands much better why people support the death penalty, and she is able to carry out her advocacy with a greater sensitivity to the needs and beliefs of those who do not agree with her. Her relativism, in turn, lends credibility to her work. Dismissing the other side of the argument as totally without merit can be too easy—it is far more useful to understand the nature of the controversy and the reasons *why* the issue defies resolution.

The most controversial issues of all are often those that center on a constitutional right. The Bill of Rights—the first ten amendments to the U.S. Constitution—spells out some of the most fundamental rights that distinguish the governmental system of the United States from those that allow fewer (or other) freedoms. But the sparsely worded document is open to interpretation, and clauses of only a few words are often at the heart of national debates. The Bill of Rights was meant to protect individual liberties; but the needs of some individuals clash with those of society as a whole, and when this happens someone has to decide where to draw the line. Thus the Constitution becomes a battleground between the rights of individuals to do as they please and the responsibility of the government to protect its citizens. The First Amendment's guarantee of "freedom of speech," for example, leads to a number of difficult questions. Some forms of expression, such as burning an American flag, lead to public outrage—but nevertheless are said to be protected by the First Amendment. Other types of expression that most people find objectionable, such as sexually explicit material involving children, are not protected because they are considered harmful. The question is not only where to draw the line, but how to do this without infringing on the personal liberties on which the United States was built.

The Bill of Rights raises many other questions about individual rights and the societal "good." Is a prayer before a high school football game an "establishment of religion" prohibited by the First Amendment? Does the Second Amendment's promise of "the right to bear arms" include concealed handguns? Is stopping and frisking someone standing on a corner known to be frequented by drug dealers a form of "unreasonable search and seizure" in violation of the Fourth Amendment? Although the nine-member U.S. Supreme Court has the ultimate authority in interpreting the Constitution, its answers do not always satisfy the public. When a group of nine people—sometimes by a five-to-four vote—makes a decision that affects the lives of hundreds of millions, public outcry can be expected. And the composition of the Court does change over time, so even a landmark decision is not guaranteed to stand forever. The limits of constitutional protection are always in flux.

These issues make headlines, divide courts, and decide elections. They are the questions most worthy of national debate, and this series aims to cover them as thoroughly as possible. Each volume sets out some of the key arguments surrounding a particular issue, even some views that most people consider extreme or radical—but presents a balanced perspective on the issue. Excerpts from the relevant laws and judicial opinions and references to central concepts, source material, and advocacy groups help the reader to explore the issues even further and to read "the letter of the law" just as the legislatures and the courts have established it.

It may seem that some debates—such as those over capital punishment and abortion, debates with a strong moral component— will never be resolved. But American history offers numerous examples of controversies that once seemed insurmountable but now are effectively settled, even if only on the surface. Abolitionists met with widespread resistance to their efforts to end slavery, and the controversy over that issue threatened to cleave the nation in two; but today public debate over the merits of slavery would be unthinkable, though racial inequalities still plague the nation. Similarly unthinkable at one time was suffrage for women and minorities, but this is now a matter of course. Distributing information about contraception once was a crime. Societies change, and attitudes change, and new questions of social justice are raised constantly while the old ones fade into irrelevancy.

Whatever the root of the controversy, the books in POINT/ COUNTERPOINT seek to explain to the reader the origins of the debate, the current state of the law, and the arguments on both sides. The goal of the series is to inform the reader about the issues facing not only American politicians, but all of the nation's citizens, and to encourage the reader to become more actively involved in resolving these debates, as a voter, a concerned citizen, a journalist, an activist, or an elected official. Democracy is based on education, and every voice counts—so every opinion must be an informed one.

This volume examines controversial issues in the area of "intellectual property." Most people are familiar with the word "property" referring to a piece of land or someone's belongings, which are examples of "real property" and "personal property." However, intellectual property can also be quite valuable and includes writings, songs, cartoon characters, brand names, inventions, and other ideas. The law protects creators' right to profit from their creations—and to keep others from doing so without the creator's permission.

Many people first became acquainted with intellectual property issues when song-swapping software became popular. Millions of people who would never dream of shoplifting a CD felt comfortable downloading songs from the Internet, even though the writers and performers of the songs did not receive any money from the downloads. Musicians and recording companies reacted angrily, calling the practice "piracy" and demanding greater legal protections. However, many have spoken in favor of new rules for intellectual property in the digital age and support expansion of the "public domain"—intellectual property that effectively belongs to everyone. In addition to song swapping, this volume looks at Congress's decision to extend the length of copyright protection by many years, efforts to crack down on Websites critical of businesses, and the right of celebrities to keep people from using their names and likenesses without their permission.

What Is Intellectual Property?

When we think of the legal system and the protection of property, we naturally think of real property—land, the regulation of land uses, real-estate law, zoning, subdivisions, and other personal property. Modern law was developed in feudal times to protect nobles' private property from the monarchy. Later, it extended the right of personal property to a broader class of free men. The legal system addressed concepts such as trespass to land and trespass to chattels (certain items of property); thus, it revolved around personal, tangible property.

In the twenty-first century, another type of property has taken center stage. It is called "intellectual property," and it refers to intangible assets or rights that develop from the intellectual or creative process.[1] This can include books, computers, inventions, trade names, slogans, and much more.

Types of Intellectual Property

There are different types of intellectual property; the three most common are copyright, patent, and trademark. Other forms of intellectual property include trade secrets and the right of publicity. The term *patent* refers to a grant from the government to an inventor that gives the inventor exclusive rights to the invention for 20 years from the date of application. Patents for inventions are called utility patents, while patents for designs are called design patents. Patents for designs are given for 14 years. An invention is the creation of something new. A design refers to the unique drawing or depiction of the decorative or ornamental character of a pattern, model, shape of a manufacturing product. A person must file an application with the U.S. Patent and Trademark Office to receive a patent.

Copyright refers to an intangible property right given to authors, artists, and other creators of a literary or artistic work. Examples of copyrightable works include literary works; musical

Two Definitions of Intellectual Property

Intellectual property, or *IP,* refers to a legal entitlement that is sometimes attached to the expressed form of an idea or of other intangible subject matter. In general terms, this legal entitlement sometimes enables its holder to exercise exclusive control over the use of the IP. The term *intellectual property* reflects the idea that the subject matter of IP is the product of the mind or the intellect and that, once established, such entitlements are treated, as far as possible, as equivalent to tangible property and may be enforced as such by the courts.

Source: Wikipedia, available online at *http://en.wikipedia.org/wiki/Intellectual_property.*

A term often used to refer generically to property rights created through intellectual and/or discovery efforts of a creator that are generally protectable under patent, trademark, copyright, trade secret, trade dress or other law.

Source: Tech Transfer at the University of Michigan, available online at *http://www.techtransfer.umich.edu/index/glossary.html.*

works; dramatic creations; choreographic work; pictorial, graphic and sculptural works; films; and sound recordings. Copyrights for written work are granted for the life of the author plus 70 years. Copyrights for publishers are given for 95 years after the date of publication or 120 years after creation. Registering a copyright is not mandatory; however, for a person to recover damages for copyright infringement, the copyright must be registered with the U.S. Copyright Office.

Both patents and copyrights are protected in the United States Constitution. Article I, section 8(8) provides that Congress has the power "To promote the progress of science and useful arts, by securing for limited times to authors and inventors the exclusive rights to their respective writings and discoveries."[2] Copyrights are given to "authors" for their "writings," and patents are given to "inventors" for their "discoveries."

Not all copying constitutes a violation under federal copyright law. Under a concept known as the idea/expression dichotomy, copyright protects particular expressions of ideas but not ideas themselves. Copyright also contains a safety-valve concept for expression known as fair use. Fair use refers to a limited privelege that enables a person to copy part of another's work without violating copyright law. The Copyright Act of 1976 provides: "The fair use of a copyrighted work . . . for purposes such as criticism, comment, news reporting, teaching (including multiple copies for classroom use), scholarship, or research, is not an infringement of copyright."[4] For example, if a person writes a book review, he or she may quote from the book being reviewed. The idea/expression dichotomy and fair use are how copyright works with the First Amendment right to freedom of expression.[3]

Copyright law lists four nonexclusive factors as especially relevant in determining fair use:

1. The purpose and character of the use, including whether such use is of a commercial nature or is for nonprofit educational purposes.

2. The nature of the copyrighted work.

3. The proportion of material that was copied.

4. The effect of the potential market for or value of the copyrighted work.[5]

• **Can you name some other examples of fair use?**

Trademark refers to distinctive words, names, symbols, images, or appearances that a company or person uses to identify and market itself and its goods and services. For example, the Coca-Cola Company has a trademark in its names, "Coca-Cola" and "Coke." Famed boxing ring announcer Michael Buffer has trademarked his classic phrase "Let's get ready to rumble," which he announces at major championship-level bouts. If others want to use this phrase, they must pay a licensing fee to Buffer. Businesses that use another business's name or slogan risk trademark infringement. A trademark usually must be registered with the U.S. Patent and Trademark Office or with an appropriate state office. Trademarks are not mentioned in the United States Constitution. The Lanham Act, the major federal trademark law, was passed in 1946.[6]

Rights of Intellectual Property

The law protects intellectual property by granting exclusive rights to the holders, who can sue for infringement if others use their intellectual property. If Firm X uses or sells the patented invention of Firm Y, Firm Y can sue for patent infringement. If Book Publisher Y prints and sells copies of a book for which Publisher X has the copyright, Publisher X can sue for copyright infringement. If Publisher Y sells its product using the trade-marked slogan of Publisher X, then Publisher X can sue for trademark infringement. In copyright law, if Publisher Y photo-copies and sells copies of a book copyrighted by Mr. Author and Publisher X, then Publisher Y is committing a classic case of direct copyright infringement.

If a person directly copies another's copyrighted material, that person has committed direct copyright infringement. A more difficult question arises in cases that are not direct infringement. What if a company simply enables a third party to commit copyright infringement? If this happens, that person or company arguably has committed contributory or vicarious infringement.[7] The U.S. Supreme Court is currently considering a very important case of alleged contributory copyright infringement, also called secondary copyright infringement. In *Metro-Goldwyn-Mayer Studios, Inc., et al. v. Grokster, Ltd., et al.*,[8] more than 20 entertainment companies have sued 2 companies that enable Internet users to easily share music files in the digital world. The entertainment companies contend that these file-sharing companies, which employ peer-to-peer (P2P) software technology, contribute to massive amounts of direct copyright infringement by their users.

- **What is the difference between direct copyright infringement and contributory copyright infringement?**

Trademark law has also expanded to provide greater protection to businesses and merchants who market under protected slogans. Traditional trademark infringement claims required a trademark owner to prove that another entity used a mark that was likely to confuse consumers. In 1995, trademark law expanded to prohibit what is known as trademark dilution. Under this new law, there is no need to prove likelihood of consumer confusion; it requires the plaintiff to show only that another dilutes or lessens the distinctive quality of its protected mark. A company can prove trademark dilution by users of its mark even when the defendant's goods and services are not related to the plaintiff's use of the mark.[9]

In 1999, trademark law expanded yet again to apply to so-called "cybersquatters"—individuals who buy Internet domain names and sit on them like squatters. Some individuals purchase domain names of famous companies in the hopes of selling the domain names back to the companies for large profits. This trend led to the Anticybersquatting Consumer Protection Act (ACPA).

Intellectual property comprises more than the big three: copyright, trademark, and patent law. It also consists of the relatively new cause of action known as the right of publicity. The Legal Information Institute at Cornell provides an apt definition of the right of publicity, writing, "The right of publicity prevents the unauthorized commercial use of an individual's name, likeness, or other recognizable aspects of one's persona. It gives an individual the exclusive right to license the use of their identity for commercial promotion."[10] Critics charge that the right of publicity gives unneeded, unjust enrichment to celebrities and that it infringes on the fundamental right to freedom of expression protected by the First Amendment. Supporters counter that the right of publicity is an intellectual property right that rewards people for their labor and years of work to become famous.

This book examines four issues of conflict and controversy within the fascinating world of intellectual property. The first is whether recent copyright statutes that extend the term of copyright protection and provide protection in the form of copyright management systems alter the delicate balance of copyright between protecting a creator's exclusive rights and the public's right of access to the arts. The second is whether the hot-button issue of music piracy on the Internet should lead to a finding of contributory infringement for the companies that provide P2P software or whether P2P software should be protected much as the videocassette recorder (VCR) was more than 20 years ago. The third is whether the Federal Trade Dilution Act (FDTA) and the Anticybersquatting Consumer Protection Act (ACPA) prohibit so-called "gripe" sites in which consumers take a domain name to offer consumer criticism, parody, and other offensive comments about a trademark holder. The last issue is whether the right of publicity, which gives celebrities control over the use of their name and likeness in artistic and commercial work, can be squared with the First Amendment.

These are by no means the only intellectual property issues that face the courts, Congress, and the public. They are some of the more controversial and deeply divisive, however, and the courts often are split on these complex issues. There are no easy answers, particularly because intellectual property law constantly evolves and changes in this online world. Particular emphasis has been placed on intellectual property online, as the Internet has become the legal battleground of the late twentieth and early twenty-first centuries.

Copyright Legislation Furthers the Purposes of the Copyright Clause

"From its beginning, the law of copyright has developed in response to significant changes in technology." [11]

The U.S. Constitution provides protection for copyrights in Article I, section 8(8) which states that Congress shall have the power "to promote the progress of science and useful arts, by securing for limited times to authors and inventors the exclusive right to their respective writings and discoveries."

The language of the clause provides that Congress can decide to change copyright law to better "promote the progress" of science and the arts. This means that Congress can pass new laws that provide better protection for copyright and those who have labored to create books, musical recordings, and other works of art that deserve reward.

Copyright exists to protect artists' and creators' "exclusive right" to their work. If there were no incentive for people to profit from their creations, people would not create, and "science and the useful arts" would not progress. There has to be a mechanism to protect people who create new products, programs, films, books, and similar things.

In the 1990s, Congress passed two laws to provide greater protection for copyright. These are the Sonny Bono Copyright Term Extension Act of 1998 (CTEA) and the Digital Millennium Copyright Act of 1998 (DMCA). The CTEA extended copyright protection for 20 additional years. The DMCA provided greater copyright protection in an online world where copyright piracy is a real threat. Both of these laws were necessary and constitutional, and Congress had the power to pass them.

Congress has a long history of extending the length of copyright protection.

In 1710, the English Parliament passed a law called the Statute of Anne, the first copyright law. It provided a property right of

How the Length of Copyright Protection Has Expanded Over Time

1790   28 years (14 years from publication and one 14-year renewal term)

1831   42 years (28 years from publication and a 14-year renewal term)

1909   56 years (28 years from publication and renewable up to 28 years)

1976   Life of author plus 50 years or, in case of anonymous works, 75 years from publication or 100 years from creation

1998   Life of author plus 70 years or, in the case of anonymous works, 95 years from publication or 120 years from creation

Source: *Eldred* v. *Ashcroft*, 537 U.S. 186, 194–197 (2003).

up to 28 years for authors. The law became necessary after Parliament banned licensing laws, which had given exclusive publishing power to certain publishers. Parliament believed that these monopolies held by certain publishing companies favored by the Crown were no longer a good idea. Instead, it passed the Statute of Anne, which, for the first time, protected authors instead of publishers.

The Founding Fathers of America had learned from the English tradition. They believed that copyright protection was necessary, which is why they included the copyright clause in the Constitution, ratified in 1787. A few years later, in 1790, Congress passed the Copyright Act of 1790 for "the encouragement of learning." [12] This also provided protection to authors for up to 28 years: It gave creators a 14-year term; if the author was still alive when that term ended, the copyright could be renewed for an additional 14 years.

Congress extended copyright protection in 1831, 1909, and 1976. In 1998, it did so again through the CTEA. Congress did not pass the CTEA quickly or without consideration; the law was passed after "years of legislative consideration, numerous hearings, and a 1993 study by the Copyright Office on the duration of copyright." [13]

- **How long do you think copyrights should last?**

The CTEA is a constitutional exercise of Congress' power.

Eric Eldred, who makes classic literature available in the public domain on his Website, contended that Congress exceeded its constitutional authority in passing the CTEA. He argued that Congress slanted copyright law too far toward copyright owners and against the public. Backed by Harvard University's Berkman Center for Internet and Society, Eldred mounted a legal challenge to the CTEA. He claimed that the law was unconstitutional under both the copyright clause and the First Amendment.

Copyright term extensions in question

The U.S. Supreme Court is considering whether the 1998 Sonny Bono Copyright Term Extension Act is unconstitutional. The legislation, named for the late representative from California, extended the copyright terms by 20 years.

1998 act's main effect on copyright terms
Years after the death of the author or creator

50   70

For properties owned by a corporation, years after first publication

75   95

If the Supreme Court decides the extension is unconstitutional, here are some of the properties whose copyrights would expire soon.

Songs and compositions	Movies	Cartoon characters
"Rhapsody in Blue" "Stardust" "Yes Sir! That's My Baby"	"Casablanca" "Gone With the Wind" "The Wizard of Oz"	Disney's Goofy, Donald Duck and Pluto

SOURCE: Associated Press   AP

The graphic above shows how the 1998 Sonny Bono Copyright Term Extension Act affects copyright terms. The case of *Eldred* v. *Ashcroft* called into question the constitutionality of the Act.

The U.S. government pointed out that there were rational reasons for extending copyright. These included keeping U.S. copyright protection consistent with copyright protection in the European Union and encouraging copyright owners to invest in new ways to restore and enhance public distribution of existing copyrights.

- **Why should Americans be concerned with keeping copyright protection consistent with laws in the European Union?**

The CTEA does not violate the copyright clause.

Eldred's claims were rejected by the federal courts, including the U.S. Supreme Court. On January 15, 2003, the U.S. Supreme Court ruled 7–2 in *Eldred* v. *Ashcroft* that the CTEA was constitutional.[14] The Court noted that, throughout the history of the country, Congress has lengthened the term of copyright protection. "Guided by text, history and precedent, we cannot agree with petitioners' submission that extending the duration of existing copyrights is categorically beyond Congress' authority under the Copyright Clause," Justice

FROM THE BENCH

Eldred v. *Ashcroft*, 537 U.S. 186, 206–207 (2003)

The CTEA reflects judgments of a kind Congress typically makes, judgments we cannot dismiss as outside the Legislature's domain. . . . A key factor in the CTEA's passage was a 1993 European Union (EU) directive instructing EU members to establish a copyright term of life plus 70 years. Consistent with the Berne Convention, the EU directed its members to deny this longer term to the works of any non-EU country whose laws did not secure the same extended term. By extending the baseline United States copyright term to life plus 70 years, Congress sought to ensure that American authors would receive the same copyright protection in Europe as their European counterparts. The CTEA may also provide greater incentive for American and other authors to create and disseminate their work in the United States.

In addition to international concerns, Congress passed the CTEA in light of demographic, economic, and technological changes and rationally credited projections that longer terms would encourage copyright holders to invest in the restoration and public distribution of their works. . . .

In sum, we find that the CTEA is a rational enactment; we are not at liberty to second-guess congressional determinations and policy judgments of this order, however debatable or arguably unwise they may be. Accordingly, we cannot conclude that the CTEA—which continues the unbroken congressional practice of treating future and existing copyrights in parity for term extension purposes—is an impermissible exercise of Congress' power under the Copyright Clause.

Stephen Breyer wrote.[15] The Court concluded that there is "no Copyright Clause impediment to the CTEA's extension of existing copyrights."[16]

The majority of the U.S. Supreme Court recognized that the CTEA was a rational exercise of Congress's power under the copyright clause. The majority agreed with the reasoning in an amicus brief filed by Dr. Seuss Enterprises. (An amicus, or "friend of the court," brief is one filed by an interested person or entity that is not an actual litigant in the case.) Dr. Seuss Enterprises wrote in their brief: "The term extensions of the CTEA do provide incentives for copyright holders to further develop creative works that otherwise would not be created, as well as to distribute existing works in new forms of media."[17] The CTEA does not violate freedom of speech; rather, it adds greater incentives for creators to develop more works. Several congressmen said it well in their amicus brief in support of the CTEA:

> Ultimately, there can be no denying that Congress drafted the CTEA with care and precision. It did not pick a twenty-year extension from a hat; rather, it pegged that extension to changes in life expectancy, commercial circumstances, and evolving international norms. No narrower legislation could have accomplished Congress's goals.[18]

The CTEA does not violate the First Amendment.

The Supreme Court rejected the argument that the CTEA violated the First Amendment. The Court reasoned that copyright also has built-in protections for free-speech in the fair use defense and the idea/expression dichotomy. Fundamentally, copyright furthers First Amendment values by protecting expression, not ideas—the idea/expression dichotomy. Copyright furthers First Amendment values through the fair use defense, which allows the public to use expression in a copyrighted work in certain circumstances.

The Court also pointed out that the CTEA furthered First Amendment interests in several ways. It allows libraries to "distribute" and "display" copies of published works for "preservation, scholarship or research" purposes if the work is not being commercially marketed and copies are not available at a reasonable price.[19]

The DMCA catches up copyright law in the online age.

Congress passed a second law designed to protect copyright in an age with a great threat of digital piracy. This should not be viewed with suspicion. Congress has often passed new copyright laws in the wake of new technology. In 1984, the U.S. Supreme Court recognized that significant deference should be given to Congress when technology alters the market for copyrightable materials:

> Sound policy, as well as history, supports our consistent deference to Congress when major technological innovations alter the market for copyrighted materials. Congress has the constitutional authority and the institutional ability to accommodate fully the varied permutations of competing interests that are inevitably implicated by such new technology.[20]

The DMCA represents a recent attempt by Congress to protect copyright holders in an online world. Its stated purpose is "to facilitate the robust development and worldwide expansion of electronic commerce, communications, research, development and education in the digital age."[21] The DMCA was enacted to combat the fear of piracy of digital information. As a 1998 Senate report stated, "Due to the ease with which digital works can be copied and distributed worldwide virtually instantaneously, copyright owners will hesitate to make their works readily available on the Internet without reasonable assurance that they will be protected against massive piracy."[22]

• **How has new technology facilitated copyright violations?**

The DMCA was passed in order to combat piracy in digital form. Congress also passed the law to keep U.S. copyright law compatible and competitive with copyright in other countries. Congress wanted to implement a provision in the United States Code that would mirror provisions in the World Intellectual Property Organization (WIPO) Copyright Treaty.

A key part of the DMCA helps copyright owners by punishing individuals who create and distribute products that can circumvent a copyright protection scheme, such as a technology protection system. A prime example is DVDs. Movie producers did not release movies in digital form (DVDs) until they knew that piracy could be limited. They did this by encrypting DVDs with a program called Content Scrambling System (CSS), which prevents the unauthorized viewing and copying of DVDs.

Then, a software program that circumvented or descrambled the CSS software was developed. This program was called DeCSS. DeCSS can override the CSS security system and help a computer user commit piracy of DVDs. The DMCA prohibits individuals from trafficking in DeCSS.

Some critics have charged that the DMCA has altered the balance of copyright, in part by prohibiting circumvention devices. This is an exaggeration. Congress has previously passed legislation that prevented similar devices. For example, laws prohibit digital audio recording devices and devices that decrypt satellite cable programming.[23]

One expert defended these provisions of the DMCA by comparing them to the criminal-law concept of aiding and abetting. If you traffic in a product specifically designed to infringe on another's copyright, you are aiding and abetting copyright infringement. "It basically says, if you are a person who is going to sell products that are primarily designed or advertised for the purpose of defeating locks on my doors, locks on my works, it's a criminal act," said Emery Simon, special counsel for the Business Software Alliance.[24]

The DMCA is constitutional.

Courts have ruled emphatically that the DMCA and its anticircumvention and antitrafficking provisions are constitutional. In *Universal City Studios, Inc* v. *Corley*, a federal appeals court

THE LETTER OF THE LAW

Key Provisions of the DMCA

17 U.S.C. § 1201(a)(1)(A): The Anti-Circumvention Provision

(a) Violations Regarding Circumvention of Technological Measures.

(1)(A) No person shall circumvent a technological measure that effectively controls access to a work protected under this title.

17 U.S.C. § 1201(a)(2): The Anti-Trafficking Provision

No person shall manufacture, import, offer to the public, provide or otherwise traffic in any technology, product, service, device, component, or part thereof, that—

(A) is primarily designed or produced for the purpose of circumventing a technological measure that effectively controls access to a work protected under this title;

(B) has only limited commercially significant purpose or use other than to circumvent a technological measure that effectively controls access to a work protected under this title; or

(C) is marketed by that person or another acting in concert with that person with that person's knowledge for use in circumventing a technological measure that effectively controls access to a work protected under this title.

upheld the DMCA from attack by an individual who posted DeCSS on his Website.[25] The appeals court compared DeCSS to "a skeleton key that can open a locked door, a combination that can open a safe, or a device that can neutralize the security device attached to a store's products."[26]

The appeals court also rejected the contention that the DMCA eliminated the fair use defense in copyright law. In fact, the appeals court characterized this claim as "extravagant."[27] The court explained, "Fair use has never been held to be a guarantee of access to copyrighted material in order to copy it by the fair user's preferred technique or in the format of the original."[28]

Summary

Copyright expert Edward Samuels was right when he stated that "copyright is more important today than it's ever been."[29] Multimedia companies interested in protecting their copyrights have created a billion-dollar industry that employs millions of American workers. Intellectual property is a valuable right that should be nurtured and developed.

Some critics have charged that copyright law has tilted too far in favor of copyright holders. This is not true. Recent copyright legislation, the CTEA and the DMCA, merely attempt to further the fundamental purpose of copyright—to reward and spur more creativity and innovation by rewarding those who hold the rights to such intellectual property.

The CTEA does not perpetually extend copyrights. It merely adds another 20 years, a pattern that Congress has followed with many prior copyright laws. The DMCA is a rational response to a time when increased technology has led to more piracy, particularly online. Both of these laws are necessary to protect copyright holders, and both help the public by giving greater incentives to creators.

Another leading copyright expert, Doug Isenberg, wrote in a 2003 column that the CTEA and the DMCA "are merely modern revisions to a 300-year-old legal structure that benefits us all." [30]

Recent Copyright Legislation Threatens the Public Domain

The fundamental purpose of copyright law is "to promote the progress of science and useful arts." The U.S. Supreme Court has stated that "the primary objective of copyright is not to reward the labor of authors, but to promote the Progress of Science and useful Arts."[31] Copyright law provides a limited monopoly privilege to creators that is intended to motivate creativity. As Justice John Paul Stevens has written, however, a primary purpose of the copyright clause is "to allow the public access to the products of their genius after the limited period of exclusive control had expired."[32] The limited grant to copyright holders that is given to them in the Constitution should not be perpetual. Copyright should serve the public interest rather than just enrich creators and those who own copyrights. The limited grant to copyright holders was done in order to ensure that once copyright owners had a period of exclusive control, the material would pass into the public domain. Unfortunately, copyright law has been radically altered in favor of copyright holders to the detriment of the general public.

> • **What should be the primary purpose of copyright law?**

The CTEA and the DMCA both sacrifice the public interest on the altar of corporate and individual greed. The CTEA extends the copyright term another 20 years, depriving the public domain of many valuable works. The DMCA gives copyright holders greater control over the protection of their property than ever before.

The CTEA frustrates the purpose of the copyright clause and violates the Constitution.

The copyright clause specifically provides that copyright holders receive their rights to exclusive control for "limited times." This means that the ultimate purpose of copyright law—to promote the progress of science and the arts—is achieved by granting a limited period of exclusive rights for the author or creator, followed by his or her works' entrance into the public domain. The CTEA violates the text of the copyright clause by failing to adhere to the "limited times" language.

The CTEA unilaterally extended the copyright term an additional 20 years, depriving the public of much material that was scheduled to enter the public domain. Extending the term of copyright is nothing new: Congress has done this more than ten times. Legislation includes the major copyright laws mentioned in the previous chapter. This historical pattern of extending the copyright term threatens the delicate balance that our Founding Fathers created between the copyright holders' exclusive right and the public's right of access after a limited period.

The CTEA's history is dubious.

The legislative history of the CTEA makes its passage even more problematic. Many major copyrighted entities were scheduled to enter the public domain in the early twenty-first century, including Walt Disney's Mickey Mouse. Mickey Mouse made his screen debut in a 1928 cartoon. Because copyright protection lasted 75 years at that time, the famous cartoon character was scheduled to enter the public domain in 2003. Partly for this reason, the Disney group and other Hollywood entertainment groups lobbied Congress for another extension of the copyright law. The result was the CTEA, or, as some dubbed it, "the Mickey Mouse Protection Act." Legal commentator Chris Sprigman referred to it as "the Mouse that ate the public domain."[33] He explained that the result of the CTEA was that "tens of thousands of works that had been poised to enter the public domain were maintained under private ownership until at least 2019."[34]

> • **Should private corporations be able to influence Congress to the extent that Congress will change the copyright law?**

Aside from its dubious origins, the CTEA makes a mockery of the Constitution's "limited times" requirement. One amicus brief compared the extension to the "legal equivalent of a referee suddenly adding time onto the game clock as the final buzzer sounds, which rightly caused a national furor in the 1972 Olympic basketball game between the United States and the Soviet Union."[35]

The majority of the U.S. Supreme Court reached the wrong decision in the *Eldred* v. *Ashcroft* decision.

As the preceding chapter indicates, a majority of the U.S. Supreme Court deferred to Congress in its wisdom in passing another copyright extension. The decision was not unanimous: Justices John Paul Stevens and Stephen Breyer dissented. Justice Stevens emphasized that "ultimate public access is the overriding purpose of the constitutional protection."[36] He believed that the Court majority erred by deferring too much to Congress. He criticized the Court for "quitclaim[ing] [relinquishing a legal claim] to Congress its principal responsibility in this area of the law."[37]

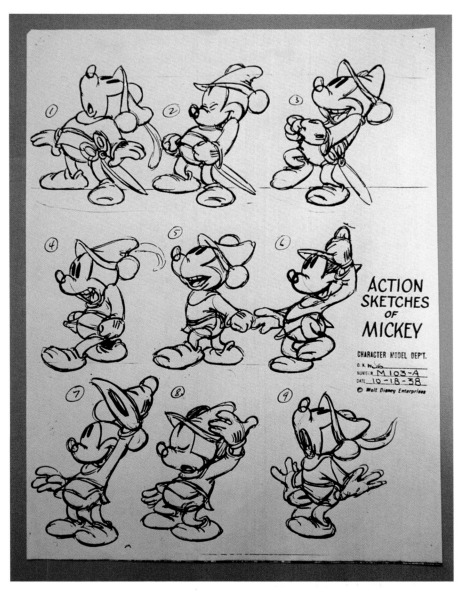

Many major copyrighted entities, such as Mickey Mouse, were scheduled to enter the public domain in the early twenty-first century. Because of this, Disney and other Hollywood groups lobbied Congress for another extension of copyright terms.

Justice Stephen Breyer wrote his own dissent. He agreed with Stevens that Congress, through the CTEA, had violated the "limited times" provision. He reasoned that Congress had made the copyright term "virtually perpetual."[38]

> • **Why do Justices Stevens and Breyer think the Court made a mistake in upholding the CTEA?**

The majority decision did offer a glimmer of hope. It did so with respect to two statements. First, the majority recognized that the lower appeals court went too far when it said that copyright laws are "categorically immune from challenges under the First Amendment."[39] This means that the Court majority believed that copyright laws are not automatically constitutional. They have to be considered against the First Amendment.

Second, the Court majority concluded that, "when, as in this case, Congress has not altered the traditional contours of copyright protection, further First Amendment scrutiny is unnecessary."[40] This means that, if a law *does* alter the traditional contours of copyright protection, then the law could be subject

FROM THE BENCH

Justice Steven Breyer's dissenting opinion in *Eldred* v. *Ashcroft*, 537 U.S. 186, 266 (J. Breyer, dissenting).

This statute will cause serious expression-related harm. It will likely restrict traditional dissemination of copyrighted works. It will likely inhibit new forms of dissemination through the use of new technology. It threatens to interfere with efforts to preserve our Nation's historical and cultural heritage and efforts to use that heritage, say, to educate our Nation's children. It is easy to understand how the statute might benefit the private financial interests of corporations or heirs who own existing copyrights. But I cannot find any constitutionally legitimate, copyright-related way in which the statute will benefit the public. Indeed, in respect to existing works, the serious public harm and the virtually nonexistent public benefit could not be more clear.

to a serious First Amendment challenge. Such is the case with the DMCA. Because the DMCA alters copyright law in a fundamental way, it is subject to a searching First Amendment review.

The DMCA is a badly misguided, unconstitutional law.

The DMCA did alter the "traditional contours of copyright protection." It did so by passing provisions that criminalized computer software that gets around a technological protection measure. Professor Edward Samuels explained that copyright has always prohibited direct copying of material and specific infringement. The DMCA, however, prohibits mere "access" to a copyrighted work.[41]

The provisions of DMCA are so broad that the music industry used them to try to prevent Princeton University Professor Edward Felten from presenting a paper on how he broke the barred access to a technological digital rights management system. Professor Felten was not attempting to help anyone pirate protected material; he was simply engaging in scholarly research. Felten stated on his blog that the "DMCA has had a chilling effect on legitimate research related to access control technologies."[42]

Copyright proponents attempt to justify the DMCA and its anticircumvention provisions by analogizing them to acts of physical theft. Their argument goes something like this: A burglar shouldn't be allowed to create a key to enter your locked doors in your home. Therefore, an online pirate shouldn't be allowed to create a computer program that blocks the copyright guard or mechanism protecting a program.

> • **Do you agree with the analogy between physical theft and digital piracy? Are there key differences?**

Professor Lawrence Lessig has pointed out that the comparisons of intellectual property to real property fail to take into account key differences: There is no right to fair use of real property, and copyright is protected for a "limited time," whereas protection for real property is perpetual. He explained:

If it is wrong to steal a car, and permissible for people to protect their property, it is wrong to crack technology designed to protect that property.

But this story about real property doesn't map directly onto intellectual property. For as I have described, intellectual property is a balanced form of property protection. I don't have the right to fair use of your car; I do have the right to fair use of your book. Your right to your car is perpetual; your right to a copyright is for a limited term. The law protecting my copyright protects it in a far more limited way than the law protecting my car.[43]

Professor Siva Vaidyanathan, author of the book *Copyrights and Copywrongs: The Rise of Intellectual Property and How It Threatens Creativity*, is even more critical of the DMCA and has called it "reckless, poorly thought out and with gravely censorious consequences."[44]

Edward Samuels

The Digital Millennium Copyright Act is not traditional copyright law at all; rather, it's a new paradigm reinforcing the copyright protection and copyright management systems that are adopted by the copyright owners themselves. The new act protects the package, rather than the content....

Copyright has always been directed at copying and other specific infringing activities, and mere "access" to a copyrighted work has never been barred under copyright. But the new act prevents not only the copying of works, but even access to works. And once access is controlled by electronic protection systems, it's impossible to get at even the parts that are supposed to be available for use by the public.

Source: Edward Samuels, *The Illustrated History of Copyright.* New York: Thomas Dunne Books, 2000, pp. 118–119.

The history of the DMCA left out the public.

Many in the copyright world feared the Internet. Some of these fears are reasonable. The problems of digital piracy, addressed later in this book, show that there was cause for some concern. For this reason, many intellectual property owners pushed Congress to pass legislation that would restore greater control and power to copyright owners. Copyright owners needed some type of digital rights management system to combat piracy. In 1995, a government-sponsored white paper (or serious research paper) entitled "Intellectual Property and the National Information Infrastructure" pushed for government support of copyright management systems that would enable copyright holders to control access to their products.

> • **Is the public adequately represented during the drafting of copyright legislation?**

Congress did this by passing the DMCA. The problem is that Congress went overboard with this act. The DMCA radically alters the balance of copyright law by giving too much control to copyright owners.

Fair use is an important aspect to copyright law. It is said to be a fundamental way that copyright law comports (works) with the First Amendment. The DMCA essentially leaves fair use out

Professor Jessica Litman

The DMCA is long, internally inconsistent, difficult even for copyright experts to parse and harder still to explain. Most importantly, it seeks for the first time to impose liability on ordinary citizens for violations of provisions that they have no reason to suspect are part of the law, and to make noncommercial and noninfringing behavior illegal on the theory that it will help to prevent piracy.

Source: Jessica Litman, *Digital Copyright.* Amherst, NY: Prometheus Books, 2001, p. 145.

of the equation with its anticircumvention provisions. There is no fair use defense to a violation of the anticircumvention and antitrafficking provisions of the DMCA.

Fearful of the demise of fair use, Representative Rich Boucher introduced a measure called the Digital Media Consumers' Rights Act of 2005 in Congress.[45] The bill contains so-called "fair use amendments" to ensure that people are not punished under the DMCA for scientific research and for the "manufacture or distribut[ion] [of] a hardware or software product capable of substantial noninfringing uses."[46]

Summary

Copyright gives a limited monopoly to copyright holders in order to spur greater creativity and innovation. The material

Jason Sheets

The DMCA also does not provide any exemptions for circumventing technological protection systems for the purpose of engaging in parody, criticism, or news reporting. In addition to these fair uses, there are many other possible fair uses and innovative activities for which the DMCA does not provide exemptions. Essentially, the statute does not provide many viable defenses.

The anti-circumvention provisions can, and will, be used to block competition and the introduction of new technologies. The DMCA protects locks that were developed for and are primarily used to exclude unauthorized third parties from reverse engineering the owner's product. Most § 1201 claims will not be raised against hackers or those intending to make infringing products; most § 1201 claims will be levied against competitors, including competitors making non-infringing products.

Source: Jason Sheets, "Copyright Misused: The Impact of the DMCA Anti-circumvention Measures on Fair & Innovative Markets." 23 HASTINGS COMMENT L.J. 1, 19 (2000).

then passes into the public domain. This means that copyright law is not designed solely for the benefit of copyright holders: Its overarching benefit is to ensure progress of the arts.

The CTEA and the DMCA tilt the balance calibrated between the limited monopoly of copyright holders and the general public. These laws ignore First Amendment principles. The CTEA ignores the stated "limited times" provision of the copyright clause and was generated by high-powered corporate interests. The DMCA ignores settled copyright law by protecting all access to works and deprives the public of fair use.

Because of these laws, as Professor Lawrence Lessig has said, "we are instead entering a time when copyright is more effectively protected than at any time since Gutenberg."[47] As this author has written, "The challenge in the 21st century will be to balance content creators' and content owners' rights without stifling the development of new technology and legitimate public access to information. Hopefully, copyright can serve as 'an engine of free expression,' rather than a limit on the First Amendment."[48]

Internet Music Piracy Threatens Copyright and Requires Greater Protections From Congress

Piracy of digital works has wreaked havoc on the entertainment industry. Millions, if not billions, of songs are transferred illegally online through new technologies that make online copying quick and easy. Peer-to-peer (P2P) software has enabled private individuals to download movies and music without paying and swap them easily and illegally. This is the online equivalent of walking into a bookstore and stealing a book or walking into a record store and stealing a CD.

Online piracy has reached epidemic proportions. The Recording Industry Association of America (RIAA), which combats music piracy, said, "Today's pirates operate not on the high seas but on the Internet, in illegal CD factories, distribution centers, and on the street. The pirate's credo is still the same—why pay for it when it's so easy to steal?"[49] One commentator reported that online piracy caused the music industry to lose 2.4 billion dollars and the film industry to lose 3 billion dollars in 2003.[50]

For this reason, the RIAA has targeted the direct infringers—those who directly infringe on copyrightable music by illegally sharing digital music files. In February 2005, the RIAA brought copyright infringement suits against 753 fire sharers. These individuals use unauthorized P2P services like KaZaa, eDonkey, and Grokster.[51]

As this book goes to press, the issue of music piracy is before the United States Supreme Court. In *Metro-Goldwyn-Mayer Studios, Inc., et al.* v. *Grokster, Ltd., et al.*, the high court will determine whether several entertainment companies can sue two companies (Grokster and Streamcast) for secondary copyright infringement. The entertainment companies allege that Grokster and Streamcast provide the essential tool—in the form of P2P file sharing software—that aids and abets copyright infringement. A decision by the court is expected in late June 2005.

> • **Do you think that providing a tool that might contribute to copyright infringement is sufficient grounds for prosecuting under copyright laws?**

The massive amounts of online copyright infringement have caused many in the recording industry to lose their jobs.

Senator Gordon Smith

It is conceivable that some consumers who first took to the Internet when many services were free may have come to expect that all services over the Internet are, or should be, free. To them, perhaps, P2P is just "free downloading." To me, it looks a lot more like "freeloading"—or taking someone else's property without paying for it.

Source: Testimony, U.S. Senate Committee on Commerce, Science and Transportation, "The Future of Peer-to-Peer Technology," June 23, 2004. Available online at *http://commerce.senate.gov/hearings/testimony.cfm?id=1247&wit_id=2230*.

The National Academy of Recording Arts and Sciences, which filed an amicus or friend-of-the-court brief in support of the entertainment companies, reports that background musicians, songwriters, record producers, sound engineers, conductors, and arrangers have been directly threatened.[52] The Academy explained in their brief: "In fact, countless members of the Academy and other amici organizations have lost their jobs with record companies, or seen their contracts not renewed, because of the dramatic downturn in the music business due to such infringement."[53]

Peer-to-peer software enables piracy.

This technological breakthrough developed with P2P. This software enables a computer user to connect to other computers and transfer data from one computer to another. If both computers use the same P2P technology, the users can upload files from each other's computers. Using P2P technology, an individual can surf the Internet for files available to be copied from other computers. The individual then downloads the music.

The software has generated intense controversy because it enables individuals to record, reproduce, and distribute music and movies from online without paying for them. The individuals who swap copyrightable music files illegally are direct infringers.

Equally as important, the companies that provide the P2P software contribute to the copyright violations: They aid and abet the copyright violations. These companies therefore are contributory infringers.

The controversy began with a company called Napster. Napster employed a centralized index system that kept an updated list of files that were available for download by Napster subscribers. The files were stored in the MP3 format, which allows the compression of large amounts of data in computer files. Users of Napster could search for music on the MP3 files of other computer users.

"What it all amounts to is a colossal CD copying party," wrote entertainment lawyer Howard King.[54] "The bottom line is that

Napster Inc. cofounder Shawn Fanning leaves the federal building in San Francisco after a federal judge shut down the Napster service, saying that the company that revolutionized music distribution was encouraging "wholesale infringing" against recording industry copyrights.

using Napster to distribute copyrighted music is stealing, and while Napster may have blocked a few hundred thousand users from doing so, the looting is going to continue. Just because fans think they can hide behind technology to take what isn't theirs doesn't change the moral or legal implications of what they are doing."[55]

Federal courts have recognized that online music piracy violates copyright laws.

The controversy over online piracy of music began with the celebrated case of Napster. Shawn Fanning, then a college freshman

FROM THE BENCH

A & M Records, Inc. v. *Napster, Inc.,* 239 F.3d 1004 (9th Cir. 2001)

It is apparent from the record that Napster has knowledge, both actual and constructive of direct infringement. Napster claims that it is nevertheless protected from contributory liability by the teaching of *Sony Corp.* v. *Universal City Studios, Inc.,* 464 U.S. 417, 78 L. Ed. 2d 574, 104 S. Ct. 774 (1984). We disagree. We observe that Napster's actual, specific knowledge of direct infringement renders *Sony's* holding of limited assistance to Napster. . . .

Regardless of the number of Napster's infringing versus noninfringing uses, the evidentiary record here supported the district court's finding that plaintiffs would likely prevail in establishing that Napster knew or had reason to know of its users' infringement of plaintiffs' copyrights. . . .

We nevertheless conclude that sufficient knowledge exists to impose contributory liability when linked to demonstrated infringing use of the Napster system. . . . The record supports the district court's finding that Napster has actual knowledge that specific infringing material is available using its system, that it could block access to the system by suppliers of the infringing material, and that it failed to remove the material. . . .

Our review of the record requires us to accept the district court's conclusion that plaintiffs have demonstrated a likelihood of success on the merits of the vicarious copyright infringement claim. Napster's failure to police the system's "premises," combined with a showing that Napster financially benefits from the continuing availability of infringing files on its system, leads to the imposition of vicarious liability.

at Northeastern University in Boston, developed a computer program that allowed him to share his music with his friends by storing his music in MP3 files and allowing others to upload those files from his computer. Fanning's program also allowed users to search the MP3 files of other computer users. He developed and marketed this program into a million-dollar business called Napster. The result was a veritable revolution that led to widespread copying of music.

Several record companies—Universal, Sony, and BMG—sued Napster for copyright violations. Musicians, including rap mogul Dr. Dre and the heavy metal group Metallica, also sued Napster. Fanning and Napster countered that Napster was protected by the fair use doctrine. Napster identified three fair uses of its technology: (1) sampling, where individuals listen to, or sample, the music before deciding whether to purchase it; (2) space-shifting, merely acquiring music they already own in a different format (MP3 files); and (3) permissive distribution by certain recording artists who believe that the use of Napster will give their musical works greater name recognition.[56]

The Ninth Circuit Court of Appeals rejected those fair use defenses and the comparison to the *Sony* decision. The appeals court rejected the notion that sampling, space-shifting, and permissive distribution were substantial, noninfringing uses. To the appeals court, the primary use of Napster was wholesale copying of entire songs without payment to the copyright holders. The appeals court determined that Napster knew that the primary use of its company was the wholesale copying of music and that Napster knew that many of its users were engaging in copyright infringement and did nothing to stop it. In fact, according to the court, Napster facilitated the copying process. The appeals court determined that Napster was likely liable for both contributory and vicarious copyright infringement.[57] Contributory and vicarious copyright infringement are two different types of secondary infringement. These forms of infringement differ from direct infringement. Napster was not the direct infringer because

Napster didn't directly copy the files. The users of Napster were the direct users. Contributory infringement occurs when someone knows of infringing activity and materially contributes to the infringing conduct. Vicarious infringement occurs when someone has the ability to supervise the infringing activity and obtains a direct financial benefit from the infringement.[58]

In the case of *In re: Aimster Copyright Litigation,* the Seventh U.S. Circuit Court of Appeals ruled that Aimster, a company that provides P2P file sharing software and instructs how to use the software to swap music files, was a contributory copyright infringer.[59] Writing for the court, Judge Richard Posner reasoned that Aimster engaged in "willful blindness" of the copyright infringement carried on by its subscribers. Posner noted that Aimster failed to show that its subscribers used its service for anything other than infringing activities.

Congress should pass the Induce Act to stop the online piracy.

Congress attempted to address the problems of online piracy with a bill called the Inducing Infringement of Copyrights Act of 2004, or the Induce Act.[60] This bill would create a new

FROM THE BENCH

In Re: Aimster Copyright Litigation, 334 F.3d 643 (7th Cir. 2003)

Aimster has failed to produce any evidence that its service has ever been used for a noninfringing use, let alone evidence concerning the frequency of such uses. . . .

Even when there are noninfringing uses of an Internet file-sharing service, moreover, if the infringing uses are substantial then to avoid liability as a contributory infringer, the provider of the service must show that it would have been disproportionately costly for him to eliminate or at least reduce substantially the infringing uses. . . . Aimster hampered its search for evidence by providing encryption. It must take responsibility for that self-inflicted wound.

violation of copyright law called "inducing infringement." The theory is that companies that are created to allow people to swap music files with peer-to-peer file sharing technology are inducing people to infringe on copyrightable materials. This law would make it easier for copyright holders to hold peer-to-peer file sharing systems like KaZaa, Grokster, and Morpheus liable for their enabling of massive amounts of copyright infringement.

Companies like Grokster and Morpheus are "deliberately dependent on infringement."[61] These companies know that the vast majority of their subscribers are committing copyright

The Induce Act

SECTION 1. SHORT TITLE.
This Act may be cited as the "Inducing Infringement of Copyrights Act of 2004".

SEC. 2. INTENTIONAL INDUCEMENT OF COPYRIGHT INFRINGEMENT.
Section 501 of title 17, United States Code, is amended by adding at the end the following:

(g) (1) In this subsection, the term "intentionally induces" means intentionally aids, abets, induces, or procures, and intent may be shown by acts from which a reasonable person would find intent to induce infringement based upon all relevant information about such acts then reasonably available to the actor, including whether the activity relies on infringement for its commercial viability.

(2) Whoever intentionally induces any violation identified in subsection (a) shall be liable as an infringer.

(3) Nothing in this subsection shall enlarge or diminish the doctrines of vicarious and contributory liability for copyright infringement or require any court to unjustly withhold or impose any secondary liability for copyright infringement.

violations. For instance, in the *Grokster* case, which is pending before the U.S. Supreme Court as this book goes to press, it has been established that 90 percent of users are using the P2P technology (Grokster) to commit copyright infringement.

> • **Do you think Congress should pass an Induce Act to address the music piracy problem?**

Peer-to-peer file sharing software should not be outlawed. Indeed, it is important technology. Still, businesses should not be able to capitalize on this revolutionary technology by engaging in practices where they derive their income and build their business on infringing activities.

There is no First Amendment free speech right to steal music.

The First Amendment, the first 45 words of the Bill of Rights, provides citizens protection from government infringements on their freedom of expression. The First Amendment does not provide a license to steal someone else's copyrightable work.

National Academy of Recording Arts and Sciences

The euphemism "file sharing" does not effectively capture the true nature of the infringing activity, which involves unauthorized reproduction of the entirety of numerous copyrighted works and the distribution of copies to others, who are equally capable of copying and retransmitting them, ad infinitum.... If the public is allowed to copy and distribute sound recordings without compensating the creators (and those who work for them), artists' principal means of support will vanish. The destructive consequences to our culture will follow as certainly as night will follow day.

Source: Amicus Brief of National Academy of Recording Arts and Sciences et al. in *Metro-Goldwyn-Mayer Studios, Inc., et al.* v. *Grokster, Ltd., et al.* (04-480), pp. 11, 22.

As Ken Paulson, the former executive director of the First Amendment Center, said, "The First Amendment guarantees freedom of music—not free music."[62] Paulson explained, "The whole concept of copyright was designed to encourage the creative process by providing some monetary incentive. . . . If an author or songwriter can have his or her work pirated without compensation, the creative process is short-circuited."[63]

Downloading music off the Internet without paying for it is the online equivalent of breaking into a music store and stealing CDs. As Judge Richard Posner wrote, the First Amendment does not give one the right "to copy, or enable the copying of, other people's music."[64]

Summary

Online piracy has reached epidemic proportions. Peer-to-peer technology is not evil; it is a positive technological development. But, some companies have used the technology and turned a willful blind eye to rampant copyright infringement. They have enabled millions of individuals to download music without paying for it, and this piracy has caused a drop in music sales. The U.S. Supreme Court should send a strong message in the *Grokster* case that such contributory infringement will not be legalized or given a free pass. Congress could also wade into these troubled waters and pass legislation such as the Induce Act, which would make it easier to go after businesses that allow people to commit copyright infringement. Copyright law needs extra protection in the digital age.

Peer-to-Peer Technology Is Valuable

Overprotecting intellectual property is as harmful as underprotecting it. Creativity is impossible without a rich public domain.[65]
—Judge Alex Kozinski

Yet, in the last four years, virtually overnight, millions of Americans found themselves branded criminals and threatened with outrageous penalties and personal bankruptcy for conduct that has been widespread and accepted for almost fifty years.[66]
—Amicus Brief of Law Professors,
Metro-Goldwyn-Mayer Studios, Inc. et al. v. Grokster, Ltd.

The media conglomerates that own many copyrights have argued against new technologies for years. They exaggerate the dangers of the new technology and the harm that they allegedly suffer because of supposed copyright abuse epidemics. These "the sky is falling" arguments should fall on deaf ears.

In the words of former U.S. Supreme Court Justice Oliver Wendell Holmes, "a page of history is worth a volume of logic."[67] The history of copyright and technology shows that copyright owners often attempt to thwart technological innovation in order to protect their profit margins. They don't care about the public good and public access to information. Such is the case with the battle over peer-to-peer music file sharing software.

Consider that, in the early 1980s, many major copyright holders railed against the videocassette recorder (VCR) as an evil that would destroy the entertainment industry's profit. Jack Valenti, president of the Motion Picture Association of America (MPAA), called the VCR the "Boston Strangler" of the film industry. Instead, the VCR contributed mightily to the coffers of the entertainment companies.

The VCR also led to a Supreme Court ruling that provided much-needed protection for developing technology. In *Sony Corporation of America* v. *Universal City Studios, Inc., et al.,* copyright owners of various television programs sued Sony, the maker of the Betamax VCR, for copyright violations. The copyright owners alleged that Sony was liable for the copyright infringement allegedly committed by certain owners of VCRs. Evidence showed at trial established that the primary use by most VCR consumers was taping television shows to watch at a later time. This practice is called "time-shifting."

A federal trial court dismissed the copyright owners' claims. The trial court noted that Sony may have constructive knowledge that some purchasers would use the VCR to commit copyright violations; however, it also determined that Sony merely sold "a product capable of a variety of uses, some of them allegedly infringing."

Universal Studios and Walt Disney Productions appealed to the Ninth U.S. Circuit Court of Appeals, based in San Francisco. The Ninth Circuit reversed the district court, finding that VCRs are sold "for the primary purpose of reproducing television programming." The appeals court reasoned that copying copyrightable material was either "the most conspicuous use" or a "major use" of the VCR, thus ruling against Sony.

> • **Do you think that VCR owners use their machines mostly for purposes that infringe on copyrights?**

In January 1984, the Supreme Court reversed the Ninth Circuit decision and ruled that Sony was not liable for contributory

FROM THE BENCH

Sony Corp. of America v. *Universal City Studios, Inc.,* 464 U.S. 417, 443 and 456 (1984)

The question is thus whether the Betamax is capable of commercially significant noninfringing uses. In order to resolve that question, we need not explore all the different potential uses of the machine and determine whether or not they would constitute infringement. Rather, we need only consider whether on the basis of the facts as found by the district court a significant number of them would be noninfringing. Moreover, in order to resolve this case we need not give precise content to the question of how much use is commercially significant. For one potential use of the Betamax plainly satisfies this standard, however it is understood: private, noncommercial time-shifting in the home....

In summary, the record and findings of the District Court lead us to two conclusions. First, Sony demonstrated a significant likelihood that substantial numbers of copyright holders who license their works for broadcast on free television would not object to having their broadcasts time-shifted by private viewers. And second, respondents failed to demonstrate that time-shifting would cause any likelihood of nonminimal harm to the potential market for, or the value of, their copyrighted works. The Betamax is, therefore, capable of substantial noninfringing uses. Sony's sale of such equipment to the general public does not constitute contributory infringement of respondent's copyright.

infringement. The Supreme Court reasoned that Sony's VCR was "capable of substantial, noninfringing use"[68] and that "private, noncommercial time-shifting in the home" was such a substantial, noninfringing use.

Peer-to-peer file sharing software is valuable and a fair use.

The entertainment industry has targeted peer-to-peer technologies that enable the copying of music online. "In the 1980s, it was the Betamax and the home taping of television broadcasts; today, it is P2P file sharing and musical works," wrote a group of law professors in an amicus brief in the *Grokster* decision. "But the sky is falling rhetoric remains the same."[69] Even though the entertainment industry lost the *Sony* case, as the law professors wrote in their brief, "the dire warnings of copyright owners never came to pass—the sky never fell."[70]

Applying the Supreme Court's standard in *Sony*, peer-to-peer technology has substantial, noninfringing uses. These include distributing movie trailers, free songs, and other noncopyrightable work and sharing work that is in the public domain. P2P technology allows for the distribution of public domain materials, government documents, and copyrighted works for which there is authorization to copy. The American Civil Liberties Union (ACLU) and a host of other groups point out that peer-to-peer software assists the Internet Archive's efforts. They have described the Internet Archive "as an attempt to create an 'Internet library' to offer permanent digital access to historical collections, many of which are no longer available through traditional publishers."[71]

Some musicians use P2P technology for their own commercial purposes, such as increasing public demand for a certain album and increasing fans' interest in attending concerts. For example, artist Steve Winwood released a track on peer-to-peer networks; this caused sales of his album to multiply eightfold.[72]

Libraries and academic institutions use peer-to-peer software to further their educational missions. Berklee College of Music has made many of its music lessons available to the public for free. This software made it much easier for members of the public to view important government documents, such as the 9/11 Commission Report. Some individuals use peer-to-peer software to spread their political beliefs as far and wide as possible, and this software will be increasingly important for that purpose. The American Civil Liberties Union explains this in their brief in the *Grokster* case: "As political campaigns move online and begin to take even greater advantage of the Internet and digital technologies, it is likely that more candidates will turn to peer-to-peer technology to distribute position papers and campaign videos and to otherwise tap into the vast audience of users."[73]

Punishing users of P2P software will thwart innovation, particularly for new inventors and creators.

Punishing the distributors of peer-to-peer software in the *Grokster* case could have the negative effect of thwarting innovation and technology. Copyright law should not enter into the realm of

Natalie Koss

The music industry's strategy of targeting P2P software will ultimately become ineffective as a copyright protection strategy. It is anathema to the evolution of new technology to encourage excessive controls of technology in the name of copyright protection. Even though the music industry has the Napster ruling on its side, and for good reason, peer-to-peer networks are increasingly being used by corporations and the government to disseminate perfectly innocent, non-copyrightable data. As these "substantial noninfringing uses" grow, the case for shutting down peer-to-peer programs becomes weaker.

Source: Natalie Koss, "The Digital Music Dilemna: Protecting Copyright in the Age of Peer-to-Peer File Sharing." 5 Vand. J. Ent. L & Prac. 94, 96 (2003).

Songwriters demonstrated outside the U.S. Supreme Court while oral arguments for *MGM* v. *Grokster* were heard inside. Although peer-to-peer networking services like Grokster allow Internet users to illegally download music and movies, the Supreme Court expressed reservations over allowing entertainment companies to sue the makers of such software in case the threat of such legal action might stifle Web innovation.

product control. Creators of technology generally should not be responsible for the illegal actions of others, particularly when there are substantial noninfringing uses of that technology. If the entertainment industry's logic were taken to the extreme, then no new technology should be allowed to develop for fear that some third parties will commit copyright infringement.

Justice Stephen Breyer appeared to understand this potential thorny problem when he posed this question during oral arguments in the *Grokster* case on March 29, 2005. He asked Donald Verrilli, the attorney for the petitioner entertainment industries, the following question:

> All right, on your test, are we sure if you were the counsel to Mr. Carlson, that you recommend going ahead with the Xerox machine? Are you sure, if you were the counsel to the creator of the VCR, that you could recommend, given the use, copying movies, that we should ever have a VCR? Are you sure that you could recommend to the iPod inventor that he could go ahead and have an iPod, or, for that matter, Gutenberg the press? I mean, you see the problem?[74]

Justice Antonin Scalia raised a similar point during oral arguments when he questioned whether an inventor should have to speculate as to the amount of legal and illegal uses of his technological creation: "I know I'm going to get sued right away, before I have a chance to build up a business."[75] Justice Scalia raised an interesting point in that society needs a legal framework that encourages innovation. The ACLU writes persuasively in their brief in the *Grokster* case: "Free speech and the public interest would best be served by rules that allow new and innovative mediums of communication to develop and flourish."[76] The government should not hamper the development of a new technology that has already demonstrated many substantial, noninfringing uses.

Author Lawrence Lessig has written that the power of these P2P file sharing technologies is their potential "to expand the power of searching technologies beyond their presently limited scope."[77] The ACLU makes a similar point: "Peer-to-peer networks are also being utilized by individuals to express and disseminate their political views and beliefs to as many people as possible, and to provide the public with access to a vast assortment of government information and political speech."[78]

• **Have you ever used a peer-to-peer network? How did you use it?**

The Eagle Forum

In many ways, peer-to-peer technology is the printing press of the Internet in distributing massive amounts of material quickly and cheaply to the world, and First Amendment interests are at stake.

The action sought by petitioner here is akin to enjoining Johann Gutenberg because of some unauthorized reproductions of the Bible. Unauthorized use of a technology—be it a printing press, an automobile, a firearm, or the Internet— has never justified interference with lawful uses. Such a rash action would be particularly unwise when the technology is still in its infancy, as peer-to-peer software is. Citation of alleged copyright infringement by some users of the printing press is not justification for shutting down all presses, and certainly not before their powerful legitimate uses become fully apparent.

For good reason this Court has been reluctant to create and impose contributory or secondary liability for copyright infringement. This Court should decline the invitation presented here to foray into contributor liability in connection with a new, still-developing technology that facilitates the exchange of information. The quickly changing technology will be different before the ink is dry on the opinion in this case, and it will be years before this Court has the opportunity to refine its holding here. Legislating from the bench is unjustified in general, and is particularly ill-suited to new technologies that facilitate protected speech and association.

Source: Eagle Forum Education and Legal Defense Fund, amicus brief in *Metro-Goldwyn-Mayer Studios, Inc., et al. v. Grokster, Ltd., et al.*, pp. 3–4. Available online at *http://news.findlaw.com/hdocs/docs/mpaa/eagle022305brf.pdf*.

Rather than thwart the development of new technology, the music industry should work toward creating a technological solution. The success of programs such as Apple's iTunes might encourage the entertainment industry to come up with creative solutions rather than heavy-handed attempts to impede technological developments.

The danger is that, if Congress rules against Grokster and Streamcast in this case, it could negatively affect the development of many new technologies. A decision against the distributors of P2P software could create legal uncertainties for other companies and designers who are fearful of being sued by media conglomerates. Inventors, engineers, and developers of new products cannot predict the primary uses of their products or whether most users will engage in copyright infringement.[79]

Emerging Technology Companies

Petitioners' proposed test would stifle innovation, particularly among emerging technology companies, which are uniquely vulnerable to increased legal risk. Inventors, entrepreneurs, and investors would be unable to estimate accurately their legal exposure because it would depend on future events, including the decisions of users of the product, courts' characterization of those uses as infringing or noninfringing, the development of technical means to prevent infringing use, and the resolution of other intensely factual issues. The proposed test would create a zone of legal uncertainty that would lead emerging technology companies, already saddled with technical and financial risk, to curtail the creation of innovative products, thereby depriving the public of valuable legal uses of new technology.

Source: Amicus Brief of Emerging Technology Companies in *Metro-Goldwyn-Mayer Studios, Inc., et al.* v. *Grokster, Ltd., et al.* (04-480), p. 26. Available online at *http://news.findlaw .com/hdocs/docs/mpaa/etc030105brf.pdf.*

Summary

Some criminals use firearms to commit violent crimes, but this does not mean that guns in general should be banned or gun manufacturers should be liable for the acts of criminals. The same reasoning should apply in the case of the valuable new technology of peer-to-peer file sharing software.

Furthermore, P2P software has many substantial, non-infringing uses. It enables the transmission of public domain materials, government documents, and other materials. It could soon become a necessity in the dissemination of important political speech and a key to political campaigns. It is a technological boon that should not be sacrificed at the altar of entertainment companies' corporate greed.

It Is Necessary to Protect Trademarks in an Online World

Too many people thrive on exploiting the profits of others by taking a free ride on their intellectual property. Some do so by directly infringing on a famous trademark; others dilute the value of a trademark by blurring or tarnishing it. Still others grab domain names in an online squatters' race. All of these phenomena can violate federal and state laws designed to protect intellectual property rights online. Fortunately, there are laws that provide recourse for people whose trademarks have been harmed or diluted by others.

Trademark law has expanded.

The modern era of trademark protection began in 1946 with the passage of the Lanham Act. The law was named after Congressman Fritz Lanham of Texas, who, in 1945, introduced legislation that eventually became the Lanham Act. This law defines trademark as "any word, name, symbol, device or any combination thereof adopted by a manufacturer to identify his goods and distinguish them from those manufactured or sold by others."[80]

Originally, trademark protection addressed situations in which someone tried to infringe on another's trademark or pass it off as his or her own. The Lanham Act prohibited commercial use of marks that are "likely to cause confusion, or to cause mistake or to deceive."[81] A classic case for trademark infringement requires the owner of the trademark to show that the infringing entity creates consumer confusion. It often was hard for a trademark owner to show that a competitor's business name created actual confusion with his or her protected mark.

To protect their intellectual property rights, individuals can register a trademark with the Patent and Trademark Office or simply engage in actual use of their mark. Individuals do not have to register a trademark with the federal government to establish rights to a mark but federal registration provides certain benefits, such as creating a legal presumption of ownership across the country. Trademark registration terms last for ten years and can be renewed for ten-year periods. The registration symbol ® means that the mark has been registered with the Patent and Trademark Office. If a person has not registered with the federal office, they may use either a "TM" (trademark) or "SM" (service mark) to alert others they are asserting trademark rights.

In 1995, Congress amended the trademark law to provide a claim for trademark dilution. *Dilution* is defined in 15 U.S.C. § 1127 as "the lessening of the capacity of a famous mark to identify and distinguish goods or services, regardless of the presence or absence of—

(1) competition between the owner of the famous mark and other parties or

(2) likelihood of confusion, mistake, or deception."

Internet trademark suits heat up

While Web search engines like Google make millions selling ad space next to the results of specific key word searches, trademark holders want laws to prevent competitors from advertising next to search results of their protected brands.

Estee Lauder sues Excite and iBeauty claiming its brand triggers iBeauty's ads in searches.	Playboy suit dismissed saying Netscape and Excite made "fair use" of its brands.	A French court orders Google to stop using the trade- marks of an online travel firm as search terms.	American Blind sues Google as well as four other sites that used Google.	Google announces a policy change to sell any U.S or Canadian trademark as a search term.

1999	**2000**	**2001**	**2002**	**2003**	**2004**

Playboy sues Netscape and Excite because "Playboy" and "Playmate" searches link to rivals' ads.	Estee Lauder drops its suit after the iBeauty agrees to drop Lauder's brand as a search term.	Goods maker Louis Vuitton sues Google. Dismissal of Playboy suit overturned, ruling sponsored links can infringe trademarks. Netscape and Playboy settle shortly after.	First hearing scheduled in AXA vs. Google which accuses Google of letting advertisers hijack insurer AXA's trademarks.

AP

Under the FTDA, a trademark owner may sue if an alleged infringer has used that trademark commercially. The above graphic illustrates a rise in such suits, which has coincided with the increasing use of the Internet for marketing.

A committee report in the House of Representatives explained that the purpose of the new measure "is to protect famous trademarks from subsequent uses that blur the distinctiveness of the mark or tarnish or disparage it, even in the absence of a likelihood of confusion."[82] Congress noted that someone should not be able to make use of "DUPONT shoes, BUICK aspirin or KODAK pianos."[83]

A person who sues under the FTDA must show (1) ownership of a famous trademark; (2) commercial use of that trademark by the alleged infringer; (3) commercial use by the infringer that occurs after the trademark became famous; and (4) dilution of the distinctive quality of the trademark. The FTDA requires that the owner of a famous and distinctive trademark show that the infringing individual or business is using its mark for a commercial purpose.

Some cybergriping sites violate the federal trademark dilution act.

Say an up-and-coming entrepreneur wants to start an Internet business. Part of his business plan must be to attract people to his Website. He thinks that he can attract many people by piggybacking on a famous trademark. He decides to do so by creating a site that contains a famous business's name with "sucks.com" at the end. He attempts to defend his use of the famous trademark by claiming that the addition of the word "sucks" is noncommercial parody protected by the Constitution. He may offer products of his own on his site in addition to consumer commentary. He may have hyperlinks on his Website that lead consumers to other products. In other words, he may be trying to disguise his own commercial agenda by hiding behind the First Amendment. This is an example of what attorney Daniel Prince has referred to as "a cleverly veiled attempt at capitalizing off the commercial magnetism of a famous trademark."[84]

Cybercriticism can violate the FTDA if it causes consumers to think of the famous trademark and then offers the sale of other goods or services. In other words, if "www.famousbusiness-sucks.com" attracts people to the site because they think of "Famous Business," the owner of "famousbusinesssucks.com" should not be able to profit off of the exploitation.

Federal courts have protected companies from cybersquatters.

The FTDA was not enough to combat the problem of people who sought to profit by the use of others' names online. Some online squatters would purchase domain names of famous companies, and many of these cybersquatters, as they came to be known, did not violate the dilution law because they did not engage in commercial use. Instead, many simply sat on the domain name, hoping to sell it back the company associated with the domain name.

Cybersquatting became such a problem that Congress amended the federal trademark statute by passing the Anticybersquatting and Consumer Protection Act of 1999 (ACPA). One

THE LETTER OF THE LAW

Text of the Anticybersquatting Consumer Protection Act

d) Cyberpiracy prevention

A person shall be liable in a civil action by the owner of a mark, including a personal name which is protected as a mark under this section, if, without regard to the goods or services of the parties, that person—

(i) has a bad faith intent to profit from that mark, including a personal name which is protected as a mark under this section;

and

(ii) registers, traffics in, or uses a domain name that—

(I) in the case of a mark that is distinctive at the time of registration of the domain name, is identical or confusingly similar to that mark;

Source: Anti-Cybersquatting Consumer Protection Act of 1999, 15 U.S.C. § 1125(d).

federal appeals court referred to cybersquatting as "the Internet version of a land grab." [85] Another commentator referred to the passage of the ACPA as bringing "some law and order to the Wild West of the Internet." [86]

A key element in the statute is whether the alleged cyber-squatter has a "bad faith intent to profit" from the trademarked business name. The statute lists nine different factors that courts may use to determine whether a company acted in "bad faith." These factors vary considerably, and courts apply them differently.

Several federal court decisions have granted relief under the ACPA. In 1996, the company Virtual Works registered the domain name vw.net with Network Solutions, Inc. (NSI), the agency authorized by the government to register domain names. Two members of Virtual Works knew that some Internet users might believe that vw.net was affiliated with Volkswagen, the automobile giant. In 1998, Volkswagen offered to buy the domain name.

Virtual Works responded that, unless Volkswagen bought the domain name, Virtual Works would sell the domain name to the highest bidder. Volkswagen sought to obtain the domain name through NSI's dispute resolution system. Eventually, Volkswagen countersued Virtual Works, claiming trademark dilution, trademark infringement, and cybersquatting.

A federal trial judge determined that Virtual Works violated the anticybersquatting statute. The Fourth U.S. Circuit Court of Appeals agreed with the lower court. "Virtual Works knew it was registering a domain name bearing strong resemblance to a federally protected trademark," the Fourth Circuit wrote. "And it did so, at least in part, with the idea of selling the site for a lot of money to the mark's owner." [87]

Cybersquatters cannot hide behind the First Amendment and the parody defense.

In another decision, a federal appeals court ruled in favor of the People for the Ethical Treatment of Animals (PETA), a famous animal-rights group. PETA sued an online entrepreneur who had the Web address www.peta.org. In this case, "PETA" stood for "People Eating Tasty Animals." The owner of the address, Michael Doughney, claimed a First Amendment defense of parody. According to him, his site merely parodied PETA.

THE LETTER OF THE LAW

What Is Bad Faith Under the ACPA?

(B) (i) In determining whether a person has a bad faith intent described under subparagraph (A), a court may consider factors such as, but not limited to—

    (I)   the trademark or other intellectual property rights of the person, if any, in the domain name;

    (II)   the extent to which the domain name consists of the legal name of the person or a name that is otherwise commonly used to identify that person;

    (III)   the person's prior use, if any, of the domain name in connection with the bona fide offering of any goods or services;

    (IV)   the person's bona fide noncommercial or fair use of the mark in a site accessible under the domain name;

    (V)   the person's intent to divert consumers from the mark owner's online location to a site accessible under the domain name that could harm the goodwill represented by the mark, either for commercial gain or with the intent to tarnish or disparage the mark, by creating a likelihood of confusion as to the source, sponsorship, affiliation, or endorsement of the site;

    (VI)   the person's offer to transfer, sell, or otherwise assign the domain name to the mark owner or any third party for financial gain without having used, or having an intent to use, the domain

A federal appeals court ruled that Doughney must use domain names that are not "confusingly similar": "Looking at Doughney's domain name alone, there is no suggestion of a parody. The domain name peta.org simply copies PETA's mark, conveying the message that it is related to PETA."[88]

name in the bona fide offering of any goods or services, or the person's prior conduct indicating a pattern of such conduct;

(VII) the person's provision of material and misleading false contact information when applying for the registration of the domain name, the person's intentional failure to maintain accurate contact information, or the person's prior conduct indicating a pattern of such conduct;

(VIII) the person's registration or acquisition of multiple domain names which the person knows are identical or confusingly similar to marks of others that are distinctive at the time of registration of such domain names, or dilutive of famous marks of others that are famous at the time of registration of such domain names, without regard to the goods or services of the parties; and

(IX) the extent to which the mark incorporated in the person's domain name registration is or is not distinctive and famous within the meaning of subsection (c)(1) of this section.

(ii) Bad faith intent described under subparagraph (A) shall not be found in any case in which the court determines that the person believed and had reasonable grounds to believe that the use of the domain name was a fair use or otherwise lawful.

Source: 15 U.S.C. § 1125(d)(1)(B).

- **Why did the court rule in favor of PETA?**

ACPA should apply to cybergripers who harm the goodwill of the company.

One of the factors relevant under ACPA is whether the cyber-griper intends to "divert consumers from the mark owner's online location to a site accessible under the domain name that

FROM THE BENCH

Coca-Cola Company v. *Purdy*, 382 F.3d 774 (8th Cir. 2004)

Purdy argues that the First Amendment entitles him to use the domain names at issue to attract Internet users to websites containing political expression and criticism of the plaintiffs. There is no dispute here about whether the First Amendment protects Purdy's right to use the Internet to protest abortion and criticize the plaintiffs or to use expressive domain names that are unlikely to cause confusion....The question raised in this case is whether the First Amendment protects a misleading use of plaintiff's marks in domain names to attract an unwitting and possibly unwilling audience to Purdy's message. Use of a famous mark in this way could be seen as the information superhighway equivalent of posting a large sign bearing a McDonald's logo before a freeway exit for the purpose of diverting unwitting travelers to an antiabortion rally.

The use of trademarks has not been protected where it is likely to create confusion as to the source or sponsorship of the speech or goods in question. ...Just because an opponent of the war in Iraq might assert an expressive purpose in creating the website with the name lockheedmartin.com, for example, the First Amendment would not grant him the right to use a domain name confusingly similar to Lockheed's mark. While Purdy has the right to express his message over the Internet, he has not shown that the First Amendment protects his appropriation of plaintiff's marks in order to spread his message by confusing Internet users into thinking they are entering one of the plaintiff's websites.

could harm the goodwill represented by the mark, either for commercial gain or with the intent to tarnish or disparage the mark, by creating a likelihood of confusion as to the source, sponsorship, affiliation, or endorsement of the site."

Many cybergripers' entire purpose with their "sucks.com" Websites is to "tarnish or disparage the mark" of a famous trademark holder. The cybergripers want to bring down the business. Also, cybergriping sites can be challenged if they convey false information that harms the reputation of the company that they are criticizing. Cybergripers thus are subject to defamation laws.

Summary

Trademark law protects businesses and spurs the growth of our capitalist economy. Businesses should be able to concentrate on developing better goods and services rather than battling pirates who seek to free-ride on or exploit their good name. For this reason, Congress passed the Lanham Act and later amended it with the FTDA and the ACPA.

These laws must be enforced to prevent malcontents, rogues, and unfair competitors from free-riding on the hard work of others. Many so-called "cybergripers" have commercial agendas and seek to disparage and tarnish the good business names of others. These cybergripers hide behind the First Amendment, but they should be held accountable for violating intellectual property laws.

Trademark Laws Should Not Prevent Consumer Commentary

Trademark laws serve a valuable purpose to protect businesses from competitors who engage in unfair trade practices and seek to profit commercially off of another's intellectual property. Not all uses of a trademarked name are commercial, however. In fact, many such uses today, in the online age, deal with consumer commentary. The FTDA and the ACPA should not be used to silence critical consumer commentary. The major trademark law, the Lanham Act, applies largely to commercial speech; it does not apply to political and other forms of noncommercial speech. Cybercriticism that refers to a trademark is protected by the First Amendment.

Unfortunately, many consumers have found themselves on the receiving end of cease-and-desist letters that tell them that they must stop criticizing businesses on their personal

Websites. This happens particularly when they have created a Website that uses a business name with "sucks.com" on the end. Many have faced federal lawsuits for creating and operating such Websites.

Legal commentator Hannibal Travis correctly noted that, "given its ever-expanding reach, trademark law has the potential to operate as perhaps the most powerful instrument, other than copyright law, of public or private censorship of the Internet."[89] Even if consumer critics prevail in court, they lose, given the enormous legal costs and aggravation associated with legal defense.

- **Should trademark law be applied to noncommercial speech?**

Professor Hannibal Travis

The deterrence effect of overbroad trademark infringement doctrines not only dampens speech questioning brand images and consumerist ideology, but also the provision by others of print pages and broadcast time to such speakers. Many non-competitive users of trademarks in artistic, cultural, and political speech have finally prevailed in court only after incurring massive costs. Such costs, including attorney's fees, the costs of expert witnesses, lost time, and uncertainty can deter both lawful and unlawful conduct—indeed, the specter of such expenses is part of traditional deterrence analysis. A large number of rather frivolous trademark infringement claims have been litigated all the way up to the federal appellate courts.

Source: Hannibal Travis, "The Battle for Mindshare: The Emerging Consensus That the First Amendment Protects Corporate Criticism and Parody on the Internet." 10 Va. J.L. & Tech. 3, p. 26 (2005).

Noncommercial speech is exempt from Lanham Act claims.

The Lanham Act recognizes a noncommercial use exception for claims of trademark dilution. The law provides:

> (4) The following shall not be actionable under this section:
>
> (A) Fair use of a famous mark by another person in comparative commercial advertising or promotion to identify the competing goods or services of the owner of the famous mark.
>
> (B) Noncommercial use of a mark.
>
> (C) All forms of news reporting and news commentary.[90]

The point of dilution law is to prohibit a person from blurring the distinctiveness of a famous mark or from tarnishing or disparaging a mark. Congress opined that the use of DuPont shoes, Buick aspirin, and Kodak pianos would be examples of dilution. A federal appeals court explained that "Tylenol snowboards, Netscape sex shops and Harry Potter dry cleaners would all weaken the commercial magnetism of these marks and diminish the ability to evoke their original associations."[91]

Kodak pianos would use the Kodak trademark to attract customer attention for commercial purposes—to free ride on the good commercial reputation established by Kodak cameras. Such is not the case with a cybergriper site. The Restatement of the Law (Third), Unfair Competition, a highly influential secondary legal source (or, a source that explains the law), provides in § 25(2):

> One who uses a designation that resembles the trademark, trade name, collective mark, or certification mark of

another, not in a manner that is likely to associate the other's mark with the goods, services, or business of the actor, but rather to comment on, criticize, ridicule, parody, or disparage the other or the other's goods, services, business, or mark, is subject to liability without proof of a likelihood of confusion only if the actor's conduct meets the requirements of a cause of action for defamation, invasion of privacy, or injurious falsehood.[92]

This means that a "sucks.com" Website not used for commercial purposes would not be subject to a trademark action. Rather, it would be protected by the First Amendment.

> • **Under the Restatement view, should cybergriper sites be protected?**

Even offensive cybergriper sites are entitled to First Amendment protection.

The First Amendment provides protection for nearly all forms of expression unless they fall into categories such as obscenity, fighting words, child pornography, or defamation. The First Amendment protects even offensive expression. This fundamental principle applies to cybergripers.

Corporations are not allowed to shield themselves from negative or offensive commentary through the use of trademark antidilution laws. "The legitimate aim of the anti-dilution statutes is to prohibit the unauthorized use of another's trademark in order to market incompatible products or services," a federal appeals court has ruled. "The Constitution does not, however, permit the range of the anti-dilution statute to encompass the unauthorized use of a trademark in a noncommercial setting such as an editorial or artistic context."[93]

The ACPA, which also amended the Lanham Act, considers noncommercial use relevant in determining whether there is the necessary "bad faith" to find a violation. The statute provides that the relevant factor is "the person's bona fide noncommercial or fair use of the mark in a site accessible under the domain name."[94] The law also contains a saving clause that provides that there is no bad faith if the "person believed and had reasonable grounds to believe that the use of the domain name was a fair use or otherwise lawful."[95]

The ACPA was designed to stop people who bought domain names of companies in the hope of selling them back to the companies for large profits. It was also designed for people who would register domain names very close to major

Restatement (Third) of the Law, Unfair Competition § 25, comment (i)

The Supreme Court has held that the first amendment allows greater latitude for the regulation of commercial as opposed to noncommercial speech. The Court's decisions permit narrowly-tailored restrictions on commercial speech that directly further a substantial state interest. There is no indication that the first amendment limits application of the antidilution statutes in the context of a subsequent use of a mark as a trademark by another. Use of another's trademark, not as a means of identifying the user's own goods or services, but as an incident of speech directed at the trademark owner, however, raises serious free-speech concerns that cannot be easily accommodated under traditional trademark doctrine. The expression of an idea by means of the use of another's trademark in a parody, for example, will often lie within the substantial constitutional protection accorded noncommercial speech and may thus be the subject of liability only in the most narrow circumstances. Although such nontrademark uses of another's mark may undermine the reputation and value of the mark, they should not be actionable under the law of trademarks.

companies' names but with small typos. This has been called "typosquatting."[96] "Legal commentator Dara Gilwit explains, the goal of a typosquatter is to divert traffic to their website and use this traffic to produce advertising revenues."[97]

• **What was the purpose of the anticybersquatting law?**

Another important factor to remember is that those who sue alleged cybergripers generally must show two elements: (1) a bad faith intent to profit and (2) the registry of a domain name that is confusingly similar to or dilutive of the trademark. Cybergriper sites should not be subject to a cybersquatting claim because there is no confusion between "CompanyX.com" and "CompanyXsucks.com" for potential consumers.

Several courts have protected cybergriper sites from trademark attacks.

Many courts have rejected trademark infringement or dilution claims filed against people who engage in online criticism. A federal court in California considered the trademark claims of Bally Total Fitness Holding Corporation. Bally's sued an individual named Andrew S. Faber after Faber designed a Website entitled "Bally Sucks." The Website dealt with consumer complaints about Bally's and its business practices. Bally's contended that Faber had committed trademark infringement and trademark dilution by using Bally's trademark name and symbol on his Website. Faber countered that the trademark laws could not be used to silence his online speech, which was not designed for commercial profit.

The federal court agreed with Faber, finding that "commercial use is an essential element of any dilution claim."[98] The court determined that Bally's Sucks was not a commercial use and reasoned that "Faber is using Bally's mark in the context of a consumer commentary to say that Bally engages in business practices which Faber finds distasteful or unsatisfactory. This is speech protected by the First Amendment."[99]

A federal appeals court also upheld the right of a cyber-critic to post a "sucks.com" site that criticized the Taubman Company. The Taubman Company was building a shopping mall called "The Shops at Willow Bend" in Plano, Texas. Henry Mishkoff, a Web designer who lived in a nearby city, registered the domain name "shopsatwillowbend.com" and created a site with that address. He claimed he originally created the site as a fan site.

When the Taubman Company discovered Mishkoff's Website, they sent him a cease-and-desist letter. The company claimed that Mishkoff was violating their trademark. He responded by registering several more domain names, including "theshopsatwillowbendsucks.com" and "taubmansucks.com."

FROM THE BENCH

The Taubman Company v. *Mishkoff*, 319 F.3d 770, 778 (6th Cir. 2003)

We find that Mishkoff's use of Taubman's mark in the domain name "taubman-sucks.com" is purely an exhibition of Free Speech, and the Lanham Act is not invoked. And although economic damage might be an intended effect of Mishkoff's expression, the First Amendment protects critical commentary when there is no confusion as to source, even when it involves the criticism of a business. Such use is not subject to scrutiny under the Lanham Act. In fact, Taubman concedes that Mishkoff is "free to shout Taubman Sucks! from the rooftops." . . . Essentially, this is what he has done in his domain name. The rooftops of our past have evolved into the internet domain names of our present. We find that the domain name is a type of public expression, no different in scope than a billboard or a pulpit, and Mishkoff has a First Amendment right to express his opinion about Taubman, and as long as his speech is not commercially misleading, the Lanham Act cannot be summoned to prevent it.

When Mishkoff refused to shut down his Website, the Taubman Company sued him in federal court.

A federal district (trial) court sided with the Taubman Company, and Mishkoff appealed to the Sixth U.S. Circuit Court of Appeals. In *The Taubman Company* v. *Webfeats* (Mishkoff's company's name), the Sixth Circuit Court reversed the trial court's decision. The appeals court reasoned that Mishkoff's critical Website was protected speech under the First Amendment. The appeals court reasoned that the use of "sucks.com" in a domain name was the online equivalent of yelling "Taubman sucks" from a rooftop.[100] Mishkoff was allowed to keep all of the domain names he had registered.

Another federal court rejected a similar trademark-based suit against a cybergriper site. In *Lucent Technologies, Inc.* v. *Lucentsucks.com,* a federal district court in Virginia dismissed an anticybersquatting claim for lack of proper jurisdiction. The court added, however, that "a successful showing that lucentsucks.com is effective parody and/or a site for critical commentary would seriously undermine the requisite elements for the causes of action at issue in this case."[101]

Parody and consumer criticism are not subject to the trade dilution and cybersquatting laws.

The FTDA and the ACPA in some instances serve a valid purpose. Some businesses have diluted the meaning of another's trademark by tarnishing it or blurring it in order to increase their own profits. Certainly, some people or businesses have seemingly bought domain names in the attempt to extract large amounts of money from the trademark holders—in violation of the ACPA. Neither law, however, should prohibit consumers from legitimately expressing their complaints about companies that have wronged them or engage in desultory business practices.

The ACPA does not allow companies, in the words of one federal appeals court, to "fence off every possible combination of letters that bears any similarity to a protected mark. Rather, it was enacted to prevent the expropriation of protected marks in cyberspace and to abate the consumer confusion resulting therefrom." [102]

There is significant evidence that Congress did not intend for the cybersquatting law to reach cybergriping sites. Public Citizen, a public interest watchdog organization, has argued that "the Senate and House Committees repeatedly insisted that companies would not be able to bring lawsuits against people who established websites using trade names for the purpose of commenting upon or criticizing companies to which those trademarks belonged." [103]

An administrative panel decision by WIPO explained in one case that "sucks.com" Websites are protected if they are criticism or parody. This case concerned whether the super- store giant Walmart could prohibit an individual from using the domain name "wallmartcanadasucks.com." The WIPO panel concluded, "Thus whether wallmartcanadasucks.com is effective criticism of Wal-Mart, whether it is in good taste, whether it focuses on the right issues, all are immaterial; the only question is whether it is criticism or parody rather than free-riding on another's mark." [104]

<hr />

Summary

Many cybergriper sites are noncommercial sites that engage in consumer criticism or parody. They are not designed to free-ride on the commercial efforts of established businesses with famous trademarks. Corporations cannot shield them- selves from criticism and parody by using the trademark laws as a sword.

The Federal Trademark Dilution Act (FTDA) and the ACPA were passed for legitimate purposes. For example, a pornographic site should not be allowed to dilute the power of an existing trademark. Likewise, a cybersquatter should not be allowed to buy domain names and then ransom them off to corporations. Citizens, however, have a First Amendment right to make direct criticism—even harsh and offensive criticism—by using "sucks.com" or other critical Websites. A reasonable observer would know the difference between a famous company and a cybergriper.

The Right of Publicity Is Needed to Defend Intellectual Property

J ohnny Carson was the king of late-night television, an entertainment icon. *The Tonight Show,* which he began to host in 1962, introduced the legendary performer with the classic phrase "Here's Johnny." Years later, a Michigan company introduced its "Here's Johnny Toilets" with the phrase "the World's Foremost Commodian." The legendary comedian sued for trademark infringement, invasion of privacy, and violation of publicity rights.

A federal appeals court ruled that Carson had a viable claim to the right of publicity. "The right of publicity . . . is that a celebrity has a protected pecuniary interest in the commercial exploitation of his identity," wrote the appeals court. "If the celebrity's identity is commercially exploited, there has been an invasion of his right whether or not his 'name or likeness' is used. Carson's identity may be

Johnny Carson, the former king of late-night television, found his reputation exploited to advertise toilets. Carson was able to sue for trademark infringement, invasion of privacy, and violation of publicity rights. The right of publicity has become an area of increasing litigation.

exploited even if his name, John W. Carson, or his picture, is not used." [105]

> • **Do you think what the business did to capitalize on Carson's fame was fair?**

The term *right of publicity* was coined by Judge Jerome Frank in a 1953 case that involved rival gum manufacturers battling over the use of baseball players' names for their ads.[106] Frank explained:

> We think that in addition to and independent of that right of privacy . . . a man has a right in the publicity value of his photograph . . . This right might be called a "right of publicity." For it is common knowledge that many prominent persons (especially actors and ball-players), far from having their feelings bruised through public exposure of their likenesses, would feel sorely deprived if they no longer received money for authorizing advertisements, popularizing their countenances, displayed in newspapers, magazines, buses, trains and subways.[107]

The right of publicity has grown substantially since Judge Frank's famous decision more thean 50 years ago. Many states now recognize the right of publicity either by statute or through judge-made common law. These state publicity laws apply not just to celebrities, although celebrities often have better claims because their names carry more commercial value. The right of publicity applies to all persons. Consider the following scenario: A business runs an advertisement with a woman's picture. The business never obtained her consent to run her photo, so the business made commercial use of the photo without compensating the person.

Traditionally, the law might provide the woman with a claim for invasion of privacy. This tort, or civil cause of action, provided that an individual could not make commercial use of a person's identity without his or her consent; invasion of privacy, however, is a tort designed to protect a person's injured feelings. This might apply to someone who is not accustomed to public attention, but a person like Johnny Carson has spent much of his adult life in the spotlight.

Johnny Carson was not concerned with hurt feelings as much as with the commercial value of his name. A person who is constantly in the public eye can hardly claim hurt feelings or indignity at seeing his or her name in print; still, he or she deserves compensation for the intellectual property value of his or her name. Achieving celebrity takes years and years of hard work, as does mastering the craft that garners public acclaim and a seven-figure salary. Furthermore, should the

Restatement (Third) of the Law, Unfair Competition, § 46 Appropriation of the Commercial Value of a Person's Identity: The Right of Publicity

One who appropriates the commercial value of a person's identity by using without consent the person's name, likeness, or other indicia of identity for purposes of trade is subject to liability for the relief appropriate under the rules stated in §§ 48 and 49.

Calif. Civ. Code Section 3344

Any person who knowingly uses another's name, voice, signature, photograph, or likeness, in any manner, or on any products, merchandise or goods, or for purposes of advertising or selling, or soliciting purchases of products, merchandise, goods or services, without such person's consent . . . shall be liable for any damages sustained by the person or persons injured as a result thereof.

Tenn. Code Ann. § 47-25-1103 Property right in use of name, photograph, likeness

(a) Every individual has a property right in the use of that person's name, photograph, or likeness in any medium in any manner.

(b) The individual rights provided for in subsection (a) constitute property rights and are freely assignable and licensable, and do not expire upon the death of the individual so protected, whether or not such rights were commercially exploited by the individual during the individual's lifetime, but shall be descendible to the executors, assigns, heirs, or devisees of the individual so protected by this part.

toilet company in Michigan be able to attract business and line its pockets by exploiting a famous person's name, voice, or signature saying?

In jurisdictions that recognize a claim for the right of publicity, the answer is no. These laws provide that a person has the right to recover for the intellectual property value associated with the use of his or her name, voice, or likeness. People have an intellectual property right to control the commercial use of their identities. This is called the "right of publicity."

Professor J. Thomas McCarthy, perhaps the nation's leading expert on publicity rights, defines the right of publicity as "the inherent right of every human being to control the commercial use of his or her identity."[108] Sometimes, critics charge that the right of publicity only protects celebrities and the rich and powerful. On the contrary, the right of publicity is a general tort that applies to all people. As Professor McCarthy writes, "The right of publicity is not merely a legal right of the 'celebrity,' but is a right inherent to everyone to control the commercial use of identity and persona."[109]

McCarthy explained that "the right of publicity recognizes legal injury because such unpermitted use causes loss of the financial rewards flowing from the economic value of a human identity."[110] Furthermore, the law does not want to reward those—like the Michigan toilet company described in the Johnny Carson example—who engage in deceitful or deceptive trade practices.

> • **What is the major difference between a right of publicity and a right to privacy?**

The Supreme Court has upheld a right of publicity claim against First Amendment attack.

In 1977, the Supreme Court decided its first and only case that dealt with the right of publicity. It involved entertainer Hugo

Zacchini, known as the human cannonball, who performed an act in which he was shot out of a cannon into a net 200 feet away. In 1972, Zacchini performed his act at the Geauga County Fair in Burton, Ohio. A freelance reporter videotaped the entire 15-second act, which was shown in its entirety on the nightly news program.

Zacchini sued for right of publicity under Ohio state law, alleging that he deserved to be compensated for his entertainment act. The news station defended itself on First Amendment grounds.

The Supreme Court ruled in *Zacchini* v. *Scripps-Howard Broadcasting* that the news media could not appropriate the entire 15-second act. The Court wrote, "Wherever the line in particular situations is to be drawn between media reports that are protected and those that are not, we are quite sure that the First and Fourteenth Amendments do not immunize the media when they broadcast a performer's entire act without his consent."[111]

> • **Should the news media be able to broadcast an entire performance without paying the performer?**

Most right of publicity cases involve a defendant who advertises using a person's likeness. The *Zacchini* case dealt with the rarer situation in which a defendant used someone's performance. Nevertheless, the case stands for the larger principle that the right of publicity is a valid intellectual claim that can survive First Amendment scrutiny.

Publicity claims often trump First Amendment defenses.

Many lower courts have recognized the right of publicity as a viable cause of action that protects important interests. In 2001, the California Supreme Court balanced the right of publicity against the First Amendment in the case of an artist who created a lithograph of The Three Stooges, the famous comedy trio, and made silk-screened T-shirts.

The artist contended that his portraits of the Three Stooges were filled with artistic choices and that such portraits were sufficiently transformative, in that they altered the expression or meaning of the original work enough, to require First Amendment protection. The California Supreme Court determined that the applicable test to determine the balance between the right of publicity and the First Amendment was an important factor in copyright fair use law—whether the defendant's work was sufficiently transformative or contained enough added creative elements so that the work did not derive its value primarily from

FROM THE BENCH

Zacchini v. Scripps-Howard Broadcasting, 433 U.S. 562, 578 (1977)

No social purpose is served by having the defendant get free some aspect of the plaintiff that would have market value and for which he would normally pay. Moreover, the broadcast of petitioner's entire performance, unlike the unauthorized use of another's name for purposes of trade or the incidental use of a name or picture by the press, goes to the heart of petitioner's ability to earn a living as an entertainer. Thus, in this case, Ohio has recognized what may be the strongest case for a "right of publicity" involving, not the appropriation of an entertainer's reputation to enhance the attractiveness of a commercial product, but the appropriation of the very activity by which the entertainer acquired his reputation in the first place.

Of course, Ohio's decision to protect petitioner's right of publicity here rests on more than a desire to compensate the performer for the time and effort invested in his act; the protection provides an economic incentive for him to make the investment required to produce a performance of interest to the public. This same consideration underlies the patent and copyright laws long enforced by this Court. . . .

There is no doubt that entertainment, as well as news, enjoys First Amendment protection. It is also true that entertainment itself can be important news. But it is important to note that neither the public nor respondent will be deprived of the benefit of petitioner's performance as long as his commercial stake in his act is appropriately recognized. Petitioner does not seek to enjoin the broadcast of his performance; he simply wants to be paid for it.

the fame of the celebrity. In other words, do people buy the T-shirts because of their artistic creativity or because they contains a close likeness of the Three Stooges?

Applying this "transformative test," the California Supreme Court reasoned that the artist's "Three Stooges" T-shirts were not transformative enough. The Court wrote:

> Without denying that all portraiture involves the making of artistic choices, we find it equally undeniable, under the test formulated above, that when an artist's skill and talent is manifestly subordinated to the overall goal of creating a conventional portrait of a celebrity so as to commercially exploit his or her fame, then the artist's right of free expression is outweighed by the right of publicity.[112]

- **Do you think the California Supreme Court made the correct decision?**

In another high-profile case, civil rights activist Rosa Parks sued the musical group OutKast after it used her name in a song title without her permission. The song contained the following chorus "Ah-ha, hush that fuss/Everybody move to the back of the bus." The song had nothing to do with the civil rights movement; in fact, it dealt with the group's meteoric rise in the entertainment industry. The group said that it has a First Amendment right to artisitic expression and could use Parks' name however it wished.

A federal district court dismissed the lawsuit, but the Sixth U.S. Circuit Court of Appeals reinstated it in 2003. The appeals court decided that a jury could reasonably determine that the song title was a "disguised commercial advertisement" that was "adopted solely to attract attention" to their song. The appeals court explained in colorful language, "The First Amendment cannot permit anyone who cries artist to have carte blanche when it comes to naming and advertising his or her works."[113]

In another high-profile decision, the Missouri Supreme Court refused to dismiss the right of publicity claims of former professional hockey player Tony Twist against the publisher of the popular comic book *Spawn*. The creator of *Spawn*, admitted hockey fan Todd McFarlane, created a villain named "Anthony 'Tony Twist' Twistelli" for his comic book.

A jury awarded Twist 24.5 million dollars, but the judge granted a judgment for the defendants. Parties can petition judges to grant what are known as judgements notwithstanding the verdict (JNOV). The party asks the judge to overrule the jury's determination because the jury's ruling was unfounded. The judge in the Twist case granted such a JNOV motion. On appeal, the Missouri Supreme Court reinstated the lawsuit and sent the case back down for a new trial. The Missouri high court said that there was sufficient evidence that McFarlane's primary use of Tony Twist's name was commercial—to attract more attention to his product. "On the record here, the use and identity of Twist's name has become predominantly a ploy to sell comic books and related products rather than an artistic or literary expression, and under these circumstances, free speech must give way to the right of publicity," the Missouri high court wrote.[114]

These famous cases demonstrate that publicity claims can survive even ardent First Amendment attacks. The First Amendment is not absolute: There is much speech—blackmail, extortion, obscenity, fighting words, and defamation—that does not receive constitutional protection.

Newspapers and other media should not be able to claim automatic exemption from publicity claims.

The news media often claim that they should not be subject to publicity claims because their use of a person's likeness is newsworthy. The press should not be automatically exempt from publicity claims, however: It should not be able to use a person's image for commercial purposes and not pay for it.

Two legal commentators explained, "Few will quarrel with the need to maintain that freedom of the press. The press, however, should not, and need not, be exempt from paying for the use of the persona of a celebrity when the use is for purely commercial purposes."[115]

Courts should not interpret the newsworthiness defense too broadly. If they do, they will take away a crucial intellectual property right. As law professor Melvin Nimmer wrote years ago, "It would seem to be a first principle of Anglo-American jurisprudence, an axiom of the most fundamental nature, that every person is entitled to the fruit of his labors unless there are important countervailing public policy considerations."[116]

Summary

The right of publicity is an important legal right that protects not only celebrities but any person whose picture or likeness is appropriated by someone else for commercial profit. The right of publicity was coined in 1953 by Judge Frank and now recognized in many states either in a statute or by the courts through common-law decisions. Publicity claims prevent others from free-riding off the hard work of others. Many people have worked years and years of hard labor to get to the point where their name and likeness has value. The First Amendment is an important constitutional right that protects freedom of expression. But it is not the only legal right in our society. Often, the right of publicity will trump a First Amendment defense. The cases of Tony Twist and Rosa Parks are just two of the more recent, high-profile examples. The right of publicity is here to stay and has attained increased importance in the field of intellectual property.

The Right of Publicity Threatens Free Expression Values

The right of publicity threatens First Amendment values by punishing individuals for the content of their creations. Celebrities have used the right of publicity as a cudgel, hammering expression from the public domain. Speakers and listeners have fundamental First Amendment rights to hear comments, view artwork, create parodies, and otherwise contribute to society. Their First Amendment interests should not be sacrificed to fatten the coffers of celebrities, who need extra financial benefits the least. Moviemakers, biographers, comic book artists, small companies, musicians, and countless others have been targeted for allegedly violating the right of publicity, a judicially created right that was born more than 50 years ago.

The right of publicity censors popular culture and threatens free expression.

The right of publicity threatens free expression values. It elevates celebrities' rights above those of the consuming public—the same public that makes celebrities famous in the first place. Law Professor Michael Madow wrote that "publicity rights facilitate private censorship of popular culture." [117]

The right of publicity places individual property rights above rights of public consumption. This development should be changed to allow greater artistic freedom. One commentator wrote, "If the laws of unfair competition and publicity continue to grow unchecked, important rhetorical resources, including images that are uniquely suited to conversation among subcultures, will be taken out of the public domain." [118]

- **Do you think that the right of publicity leads to the censorship of popular culture?**

The right of publicity obviously conflicts with freedom of expression. Artists have been sued for creating likenesses of celebrities, rappers have been sued for mentioning the names of celebrities, and comic book creators have been sued for having a character with the name of a real person. Although many of the defendants eventually prevailed in court, the lawsuits themselves placed a chill on artistic expression.

The First Amendment provides the greatest degree of protection to political, noncommercial speech. For this reason, if speech is considered noncommercial, publicity claims usually fail. Unfortunately, the U.S. Supreme Court's decision in *Zacchini* v. *Scripps-Howard Broadcasting Co.* failed to provide sufficient protection for the First Amendment in a publicity claim that arose from a news broadcast. Justice Lewis Powell wrote in his dissent that "the First Amendment protects the station from a 'right of publicity' or 'appropriation' suit, absent a strong showing by the plaintiff that the news broadcast was a subterfuge or cover for private or commercial exploitation."[119] Powell reasoned that the news broadcast was "a routine example of the press' fulfilling the informing function so vital to our system."[120]

The right of publicity does not trump noncommercial speech.

Many courts have determined that the right of publicity must take a backseat to noncommercial expression. Other-wise, an unauthorized biography could never be published without the specter of the biography's subject filing a law-suit. Publicity claims require "commercial use" or "purposes of trade." Theoretically, one could argue that newspapers and books are for "commercial use" because they are published,

FROM THE BENCH

Justice Lewis Powell's Dissenting Opinion in *Zacchini* v. *Scripps-Howard Broadcasting Co.*, 433 U.S. 562 (1977)

The Court's holding that the station's ordinary news report may give rise to substantial liability has disturbing implications, for the decision could lead to a degree of media self-censorship. Hereafter, whenever a television news editor is unsure whether certain film footage received from a camera crew might be held to portray an "entire act," he may decline coverage even of clearly newsworthy events or confine the broadcast to watered-down verbal reporting, perhaps with an occasional still picture. The public is then the loser. This is hardly the kind of news reportage that the First Amendment is meant to foster.

marketed, and distributed to make money; however, the Supreme Court has said that, just because "books, newspapers and magazines are published and sold for profit does not prevent them from being a form of expression whose liberty is safeguarded by the First Amendment."[121] NBC successfully defended its televised biography of actress Elizabeth Taylor on this basis in 1994. A California court determined that "the broadcast in question involves an expressive idea as opposed" to purely commercial speech.[122] A New York court also recognized that "the publication of a biography is clearly outside the ambit of the 'commercial use' contemplated by the right of publicity."[123] The Restatement of the Law (Third), Unfair Competition, recognizes an exception for publicity claims that arise out of "news reporting, commentary, entertainment, works of fiction or nonfiction, or in advertising that is incidental to such uses."[124]

Professor Eugene Volokh

As a critic of the right of publicity, I wouldn't mind seeing the right of publicity eviscerated this way, even as to commercial advertising. . . . The right of publicity may seem intuitively appealing to many people. The notion that my name and likeness are my property seems to make sense.

But, when applied to expression, "property" is another way of saying "legally forbidden to be another's speech." Right of publicity law has long had to confront the First Amendment problems with such an approach, and in many areas, such as biography, news reporting, fiction, and the like, it has rightly yielded. But there is good reason to think that it hasn't yielded far enough—that the right to publicity is unconstitutional as to all noncommercial speech, and perhaps even to commercial advertising as well.

Source: Eugene Volokh, "Freedom of Speech and the Right of Publicity." 40 Hous. L. Rev. 903, 929–930 (2003).

Other courts have cited the so-called "newsworthy" defense. This means that, even if the use of a celebrity's name or likeness is a matter of general public interest beyond mere commercial exploitation, many courts will find a First Amendment–based defense. For example, a federal court in New York rejected actress Ann-Margret's privacy and publicity claim against *High Society Celebrity Skin* magazine, which published a nude photograph of her from the movie *Magic*. The court wrote that "it was not for the courts to decide what matters are of interest to the general public." It explained:

> The fact that the plaintiff, a woman who has occupied the fantasies of many moviegoers over the years, chose to perform unclad in one of her films is a matter of great interest to many people. And while such an event may not appear overly important, the scope of what constitutes a newsworthy event has been afforded a broad definition and held to include even matters of entertainment and amusement, concerning interesting phases of human activity in general.[125]

Transformative works receive First Amendment protection.

Several courts have determined that works that are transformative are entitled to First Amendment protection in the face of publicity claims. In *Hoffman* v. *Capital Cities/ABC, Inc.*, Oscar-winning actor Dustin Hoffman sued after *Los Angeles Magazine* published a digitally altered photograph of him as he appeared in the movie *Tootsie*. The photo showed Hoffman wearing a silk gown and designer shoes with the slogan "Dustin Hoffman isn't a drag in a butter-colored silk gown by Richard Tyler and Ralph Lauren heels." The article, entitled "Grand Illusions," showed several famous actors wearing designer clothing.

Hoffman sued the magazine under several theories, including violation of his right of publicity. A federal district court ruled in favor of Hoffman. On appeal, however, the Ninth U.S. Circuit Court of Appeals reversed the decision, finding that the magazine's expression was a combination of political and commercial speech. The Court determined that "viewed in context, the article as a whole is a combination of fashion photography, humor, and visual and verbal editorial comment on classic films and famous actors."[126] It did not matter to the appeals court that the use of the digitally altered photos was used to increase circulation: "While there was testimony that the Hollywood issue and the use of celebrities was intended in part to 'rev up' the magazine's profile, that does not make the fashion article a purely 'commercial' form of expression."[127]

> • **Do you think Dustin Hoffman should have won his publicity claim?**

The *Hoffman* case was correctly decided and paid due deference to First Amendment principles. Even Professor J.

Restatement (Third) of the Law, Unfair Competition § 47—Use for Purposes of Trade

The name, likeness, and other indicia of a person's identity are used "for purposes of trade" under the rule stated in § 46 if they are used in advertising the user's goods or services, or are placed on merchandise marketed by the user, or are used in connection with services rendered by the user. However, use "for purposes of trade" does not ordinarily include the use of a person's identity in news reporting, commentary, entertainment, works of fiction or nonfiction, or in advertising that is incidental to such uses.

Thomas McCarthy, the leading legal authority on the right of publicity, has acknowledged that "media profit and advertising do not remove First Amendment protection."[128]

Another federal appeals court also properly recognized a First Amendment defense to a publicity lawsuit filed by a celebrity. Golfing great Tiger Woods sued artist Rick Rush for trademark infringement and publicity rights after Rush created a painting featuring a likeness of Woods after his historic win at the 1997 Masters tournament. The painting consisted of more than a likeness of Woods: It also contained likenesses of two caddies and famous golfers of years ago: Arnold Palmer and Sam Snead. The Sixth U.S. Circuit Court of Appeals ruled, "Because Rush's work has substantial transformative elements, it is entitled to the full protection of the First Amendment."[129]

The California Supreme Court determined that the creators of a comic book also were entitled to First Amendment protection from a publicity suit filed by Johnny and Edgar Winter. These blues and rock musicians, who are albinos, sued D.C. Comics, the publisher of the comic book *Jonah Hex,* after learning that the comic book contained villains named Johnny and Edgar Autumn. The comic book characters were depicted with white faces and long white hair.

> • **Do you think the Tiger Woods artwork case was correctly decided?**

The California high court determined that the comic book contained "significant expressive content" beyond the likeness of the Winter brothers. The court explained that the drawings "are distorted for purposes of lampoon, parody, or caricature, and the Autumn brothers are but cartoon characters—half-human and half-worm—in a larger story, which is itself quite expressive."[130]

Parody can also provide a First Amendment defense for

Tiger Woods, one of the world's best-known golfers, sued for violation of publicity rights when artist Rick Rush portrayed him in a painting. A federal appeals court, however, ruled that Rush's work had "substantial trans-formative elements," which meant it was protected under the First Amendment.

a publicity claim. The maker of baseball cards that parodied traditional baseball cards received First Amendment protection from a claim filed under Oklahoma's right of publicity law. The court determined that "the protections afforded by the First Amendment, however, have never been limited to newspapers and books."[131]

Summary

The right of publicity conflicts with the First Amendment. It comes dangerously close to giving celebrities the ability to monitor and control popular culture. When comic book artists are punished for using the names of real persons for characters, something has gone amiss with the legal system. Creativity is being silenced to gain more money for celebrities, creating a situation of unjust enrichment.

FROM THE BENCH

Winter v. *D.C. Comics,* 69 P.3d 473 (Cal. 2003)

First, the right of publicity cannot, consistent with the First Amendment, be a right to control the celebrity's image by censoring disagreeable portrayals. Once the celebrity thrusts himself or herself forward into the limelight, the First Amendment dictates that the right to comment on, parody, lampoon, and make other expressive uses of the celebrity image must be given broad scope. The necessary implication of this observation is that the right of publicity is essentially an economic right. What the right of publicity holder possesses is not a right of censorship, but a right to prevent others from misappropriating the economic value generated by the celebrity's fame through the merchandising of the name, voice, signature, photograph, or likeness of the celebrity.

Law professor Eugene Volokh warns that the right of publicity can threaten First Amendment values: "The right of publicity, even limited to nontransformative uses, thus diminishes the range of artistic expression that people can view, as well as the range that they can create."[132] The right of publicity should not be used to silence criticism or censor artwork. Taken too far, it can lead to censorship of other intellectual property.

What Does the Future Hold?

"Whereas intellectual property is the backbone of our Nation's economic competitiveness and the only sector where the United States has a trade surplus with every nation in the world." [133]
—Resolution introduced in the
U.S. House of Representatives (April 2005)

Intellectual property is one of the fastest-growing areas of the law. The right of publicity did not exist until the second half of the twentieth century, and trademark dilution and cybersquatting developed as concerns much more recently. Intellectual property has become a battleground on the Internet: The digital revolution has led to a global economy, and this affects intellectual property. Technological innovations and changes, particularly in a digital world, have led to concerns that intellectual property is not as safe as it used to be. People who are interested in intellectual property issues should pay close attention to how the law responds to rapid technological change.

Intellectual property is in flux as this book goes to press in spring 2005. Congress is considering the Trademark Dilution Revision Act of 2005.[134] This decision would legislatively over-rule the Supreme Court's 2003 decision in *Moseley* v. *V Secret Catalogue, Inc.*[135] In this case, the U.S. Supreme Court required trademark owners to show proof of actual dilution before being able to recover under the Federal Trademark Dilution Act. The Trademark Dilution Revision Act would amend the first act to eliminate the requirement of showing actual dilution. The House of Representatives passed bill by a 411–8 vote on April 19, 2005. The measure is now being considered in the Senate. Many have predicted that it will pass.

As indicated in previous chapters, the U.S. Supreme Court recently considered a formidable constitutional challenge to the CTEA in the *Eldred* case. It is likely that the Court will hear a case that challenges provisions of the DMCA, as well. Of course, the Supreme Court is, in spring 2005, considering the fate of peer-to-peer file sharing software companies Grokster and Morpheus. The proposed legislation and pending cases show that intellectual property issues will continue to surface as the legislative and judicial branches struggle to come to grips with emerging intellectual property issues in an online era.

Trademark Dilution Revision Act of 2005

Dilution by Blurring; Dilution by Tarnishment—

(1) INJUNCTIVE RELIEF—Subject to the principles of equity, the owner of a famous mark that is distinctive, inherently or through acquired distinctiveness, shall be entitled to an injunction against another person who, at any time after the owner's mark has become famous, commences use of a mark or trade name in commerce that is likely to cause dilution by blurring or dilution by tarnishment of the famous mark, regardless of the presence or absence of actual or likely confusion, of competition, or of actual economic injury.

Introduction: What Is Intellectual Property?

1. Kenneth W. Clarkson, Roger Leroy Miller, Gaylord A. Jentz and Frank B. Cross, *West's Business Law,* ninth ed. Thompson/West Publishing, 2004.

2. U.S. Const. Art. 1, Sect. 8.

3. David L. Hudson, Jr., "Copyright and the First Amendment." First Amendment Center Online, August 5, 2001. Available online at *http://www.firstamendmentcenter.org/analysis.aspx?id=13828.*

4. 17 U.S.C. § 107.

5. Ibid.

6. 15 U.S.C. § 1125.

7. Hudson, "Copyright."

8. *Metro-Goldwyn-Mayer Studios, Inc., et al. v. Grokster Ltd., et al.* (04-480).

9. Bitlaw: "Trademark dilution." Available online at *http://www.bitlaw.com/trademark/dilution.html.*

10. Legal Information Institute at Cornell University, "Right of Publicity: An Overview." Available online at *http://www.law.cornell. edu/topics/publicity.html.*

Point: Copyright Legislation Furthers the Purposes of the Copyright Clause

11. *Sony Corporation of America v. Universal City Studios, Inc.,* 464 U.S. 417, 430 (1984).

12. Act of May 31, 1790 § 1, 1 Stat. 124.

13. Amicus Brief of Representatives F. James Sensenbrenner, Jr., John Conyers, Jr., Howard Coble, and Howard L. Berman in Support of Respondent Ashcroft in *Eldred v. Ashcroft* (01-618), p. 4.

14. *Eldred v. Ashcroft,* 537 U.S. 186 (2003).

15. Ibid., p. 204.

16. Ibid., p. 218.

17. Amicus Brief of Dr. Seuss Enterprises, L.P., Allene White, Madeline Bemelans, and Barbara Bemelans in support of Ashcroft in *Eldred v. Ashcroft* (01-618) at p. 20.

18. Amicus Brief of Congressman at p. 29.

19. *Eldred v. Ashcroft,* 537 U.S. 186, 220 (2003), citing 17 U.S.C. § 108(h).

20. *Sony Corporation of America v. Universal City Studios,* 464 U.S. 417, 431 (1984).

21. Senate Report 105-190. Available online at *http://thomas.loc.gov/cgi-bin/cpquery/ R?cp105:FLD010:@1(sr190).*

22. Ibid.

23. Ibid., p. 11.

24. Comments of Emery Simon, "Technology vs. Technology: Should Code Breakers Go to Jail? The Limits of Fair Use and Anti-circumvention," 5th Annual Cato Institute/Forbes ASAP Technology and Society Conference, November 14, 2001.

25. *Universal City Studios, Inc. v. Corley,* 273 F.3d 429 (2nd Cir. 2001).

26. Ibid., p. 453.

27. Ibid., p. 458.

28. Ibid., p. 459.

29. Edward Samuels, *The Illustrated History of Copyright.* New York: Thomas Dunne Books, 2000. Samuels at p. 6.

30. Doug Isenberg, "In Defense of Copyright Law." GigaLaw.com, February 2003. Available online at *http://www.gigalaw. com/articles/2003-all/isenberg-2003-2- all.html.*

Counterpoint: Recent Copyright Legislation Threatens the Public Domain

31. *Feist Publications, Inc. v. Rural Telephone Service Co.,* 499 U.S. 340, 349 (1991).

32. *Sony v. Corp. of America v. Universal City Studios, Inc.,* 464 U.S. 417, 429 (1984).

33. Chris Sprigman, "The Mouse that Ate the Public Domain: Disney, the Copyright Term Extension Act, and Eldred v. Ashcroft," Findlaw.com, March 5, 2002.

34. Ibid.

35. Amicus Brief of the Eagle Forum Education and Legal Defense Fund and the Association of American Physicians, Inc., in Support of Petitioner Eldred in *Eldred v. Ashcroft* (01-618), p. 8.

36. *Eldred v. Ashcroft,* 537 U.S. 186, 241 (J. Stevens, dissenting).

37. Ibid., p. 242.

38. Ibid., p. 243 (J. Breyer, dissenting).

39. *Eldred v. Aschroft,* 537 U.S. 186, 221 (2003).

40. Ibid.
41. Samuels, *Illustrated History.*
42. Edward Felton, "Freedom to Tinker" blog, October 8, 2003. Available online at *http://www.freedom-to-tinker.com/archives/000466.html.*
43. Lawrence Lessig, *The Future of Ideas: The Fate of the Commons in a Connected World.* New York: Random House, 2001, p. 187.
44. Siva Vaidhyanathan, "Copyright as Cudgel," *The Chronicle of Higher Education*, August 2, 2002.
45. H.R. 1201 (introduced March 18, 2005).
46. Ibid.
47. Lawrence Lessig, *Code and Other Laws of Cyberspace.* New York: Basic Books, 1999, p. 129.
48. Hudson, "Copyright."

Point: Internet Music Piracy Threatens Copyright and Requires Greater Protections From Congress

49. RIAA, "Anti-Piracy." Available online at *http://www.riaa.com/issues/piracy/default.asp.*
50. Anna E. Engelmann and Dale A. Scott, "Arrgh! Hollywood Targets Internet Privacy." 11 Rich. J.L. & Tech. 3 (2004).
51. RIAA, "Copyright Infringement Lawsuits Brought Against 753 Additional Illegal File Sharers," February 28, 2005. Available online at *http://www.riaa.com/news/newsletter/022805.asp.*
52. Amicus Brief of the National Academy of Recording Arts and Sciences et al., *Metro-Goldwyn-Mayer Studios, Inc., et al. v. Grokster, Ltd., et al.* (04-480), p. 4. Available online at *http://news.findlaw.com/hdocs/docs/mpaa/naras12405brf.pdf.*
53. Ibid.
54. Howard King, "Why Metallica Sued Napster." Findlaw.com, May 1, 2000. Available at *http://writ.news.findlaw.com/commentary/20000501_king.html.*
55. Ibid.
56. *A & M Records, Inc. v. Napster, Inc.*, 239 F.3d 1004, 1014 (9th Cir. 2001).
57. Ibid. at 1014-1028.
58. Ibid. at 1014-1028.
59. *In Re: Aimster Copyright Litigation*, 334 F.3d 643 (7th Cir. 2003).
60. S. 2560 (2004).
61. Amicus Brief of The Progress and Freedom Foundation in *Metro-Goldwyn-Mayer Studios, Inc., et al. v. Grokster, Ltd., et al.* (04-480), p. 4. Available online at *http://news.findlaw.com/hdocs/docs/mpaa/pff012405brf.pdf.*
62. First Amendment Center Online, "Napster decision a copyright, not a First Amendment, decision," February 13, 2001. Available online at *http://www.firstamendmentcenter.org//analysis.aspx?id=5438.*
63. Ibid.
64. *In re: Aimster*, 334 F.3d at 656.

Counterpoint: Peer-to-Peer Technology Is Valuable

65. *White v. Samsung Electronics America, Inc.*, 989 F.2d 1512 (9th Cir. 1993).
66. Amicus Brief of Law Professors J. Glynn Lunney et al., *Metro-Goldwyn-Mayer Studios, Inc., et al. v. Grokster, Ltd., et al.* (04-480), p. 11.
67. *New York Trust Co. v. Eisner*, 256 U.S. 345, 349 (1921).
68. *Sony Corp. of America v. Universal City Studios*, 464 U.S. 417, 443 (1984).
69. Amicus Brief of Law Professors, *Metro-Goldwyn-Mayer Studios, Inc., et al. v. Grokster, Ltd., et al.* (04-480), p. 4.
70. Ibid.
71. Amicus Brief of the American Civil Liberties Union, the American Civil Liberties Union of Northern California, the American Civil Liberties Union Foundation of San Diego and Imperial Counties, the American Library Association, the Association of Research Libraries, the American Association of Law Libraries, the Medical Library Association, the Special Libraries Association, the Internet Archive, and Project Gutenberg, *Metro-Goldwyn-Mayer Studios, Inc., et al. v. Grokster, Ltd., et al.* (04-480), p. 8. Available online at *http://news.findlaw.com/hdocs/docs/mpaa/aclu022805brf.pdf.*

72. Ibid., p. 10.
73. Ibid., p. 13.
74. Oral arguments in *Metro-Goldwyn-Mayer Studios, Inc., et al.* v. *Grokster, Ltd., et al.* (04-480) (Question of Justice Stephen Breyer to attorney Donald Verilli). Available online at *http://www.supremecourtus. gov/oral_arguments/argument_transcripts/ 04-480.pdf.*
75. Ibid. (Question of Justice Antonin Scalia to attorney Donald Verilli.)
76. Amicus Brief of the American Civil Liberties Union et al., p. 6.
77. Lessig, *Future*, p. 137.
78. Amicus Brief of the ACLU, p. 11.
79. Amicus Brief of Emerging Technology Companies in *Metro-Goldwyn-Mayer Studios, Inc., et al.* v. *Grokster, Ltd., et al.* (04-480), pp. 18–20. Available online at *http://news.findlaw.com/hdocs/docs/mpaa /etc030105brf.pdf.*

Point: It Is Necessary to Protect Trademarks in an Online World

80. 15 U.S.C. § 1127.
81. 15 U.S.C. § 1114.
82. *Moseley* v. *V Secret Catalogue, Inc.*, 537 U.S. 418, 431 (2003).
83. Ibid.
84. Daniel Prince, "Cyber-Criticism and the Federal Trademark Dilution Act: Redefining the Noncommercial Use Exemption." 9 VA. J.L. & TECH. 12 (2004).
85. *Virtual Works, Inc.* v. *Volkswagen of America, Inc.*, 238 F.3d 264, 267 (4th Cir. 2001).
86. Lisa Pearson, "A User's Guide to the Anticybersquatting Consumer Protection Act," Paper delivered to the Association of the Bar of the City of New York: Protecting Intellectual Property in the Global Digital Age, October 4, 2001.
87. 238 F.3d at 270.
88. The Associated Press, "Parody defense falls flat in cybersquatting case," First Amendment Center Online, August 26, 2001. Available online at *http://www. firstamendmentcenter.org/news.aspx?id =4691.*

Counterpoint: Trademark Laws Should Not Prevent Consumer Commentary

89. Hannibal Travis, "The Battle for Mind-share: The Emerging Consensus that the First Amendment Protects Corporate Criticism and Parody on the Internet." 10 VA. J.L. & TECH. 3, P4 (2005).
90. 15 U.S.C. § 1125(c)(4).
91. *Mattel, Inc.* v. *MCA Records, Inc.*, 296 F.3d 894, 903 (9th Cir. 2002).
92. Restatement (Third) Unfair Competition, § 25(2).
93. *L.L. Bean, Inc.* v. *Drake Publishers, Inc.*, 811 F.2d 26, 29 (1st Cir. 1987)
94. 15 U.S.C. § 1125(d)(1)(B)(i)(4).
95. 15 U.S.C. § 1125(d)(1)(B)(ii).
96. Dara Gilwit, "The Latest Cybersquatting Trend: Typosquatters, Their Changing Tactics, and How To Prevent Public Deception and Trademark Infringement." 11 WASH. U. J.L. & TECH. 267 (2003).
97. Ibid., p. 269.
98. *Bally Total Fitness Corporation* v. *Faber*, 29 F.Supp. 2d 1161, 1166 (C.D. Cal. 1998).
99. Ibid., p. 1168.
100. *The Taubman Company* v. *Webfeats*, 319 F.3d 770, 778 (6th Cir. 2003).
101. *Lucent Technologies, Inc.* v. *Lucentsucks.com*, 95 F.Supp. 2d 528, 536 (E.D. Va. 2000).
102. *Virtual Works, Inc.* v. *Volkswagen of America, Inc.*, 238 F.3d 264, 271 (4th Cir. 2001).
103. Amicus Brief of Public Citizen in *The Taubman Company* v. *Webfeats* (No. 01-792987)
104. *Wal-Mart Stores, Inc.* v. *wallmartcanada-sucks.com* (WIPO)(Case No. D2000-1104)(Panelist Henry H. Perritt, Jr.). Available online at *http://arbiter.wipo.int/ domains/decisions/html/2000/d2000-1104.html.*

Point: The Right of Publicity Is Needed to Defend Intellectual Property

105. *Carson* v. *Here's Johnny Portable Toilets*, 698 F.2d 831, 835 (6th Cir. 1983).

106. *Haelan Laboratories, Inc.* v. *Topps Chewing Gum, Inc.*, 202 F.2d 866 (2nd Cir. 1953).

107. Ibid., p. 868.

108. J. Thomas McCarthy, *The Rights of Publicity and Privacy*, second ed., Eagan, Minn.: Thomson West, Vol. 1, § 1.3. p. 3.

109. Ibid.

110. Ibid., § 2:2, p. 80.

111. *Zacchini* v. *Scripps Howard Broadcasting*, 433 U.S. 562, 574-575 (1977).

112. *Comedy III Productions, Inc.* v. *Gary Saderup, Inc.*, 21 P.3d 797, 810 (Cal. 2001).

113. *Parks* v. *LaFace Records*, 329 F.3d 437, 454 (6th Cir. 2003).

114. *Doe* v. *TCI Cablevision*, 110 S.W.3d 363, 372 (Mo. 2003).

115. W. Mack Webner and Leigh Ann Lindquist, "Transformation: The Bright Line Between Commercial Publicity Rights and the First Amendment." 37 AKRON L. REV. 171, 188 (2004).

116. Melvin Nimmer, "The Right of Publicity." 19 LAW & CONTEMPORARY PROB. 203, 216 (1954).

Counterpoint: The Right of Publicity Threatens Free Expression Values

117. Michael Madow, "Private Ownership of Public Image: Popular Culture and Publicity Rights." 81 CALIF. L. REV. 125, 138 (1993).

118. Rochelle Dreyfuss, "We Are Symbols and Inhabit Symbols, So Should We Be Paying Rent? Deconstructing the Lanham Act and the Right of Publicity." 20 COLUM–VLA J.L. & ARTS 123, 156 (1996).

119. *Zacchini* v. *Scripps-Howard Broadcasting Co.*, 433 U.S. 562, 581 (J. Powell, dissenting).

120. Ibid., p. 580.

121. *Joseph Burstyn, Inc.* v. *Wilson*, 343 U.S. 495, 501–502 (1952).

122. *Taylor* v. *National Broadcasting Co.*, 1994 WL 762226 (Cal. Super. 1994).

123. *Rosemont Enterprises, Inc.* v. *Random House, Inc.*, 294 N.Y.S.2d 122, 129 (Sup. 1968).

124. Restatement (Third) Unfair Competition, § 47.

125. *Ann-Margaret* v. *High Society Magazine, Inc.*, 498 F.Supp. 401, 405 (S.D.N.Y. 1980).

126. *Hoffman* v. *Capital Cities*, 255 F.3d 1180, 1186 (9th Cir. 2001).

127. Ibid.

128. J. Thomas McCarthy, *Rights of Publicity*, §8.69.

129. *ETW Corp.* v. *Jireh Pub., Inc.*, 332 F.3d 915, 938 (6th Cir. 2003).

130. *Winter* v. *D.C. Comics*, 30 Cla. 4th 881, 890 (Cal. 2003).

131. *Cardtoons, L.C.* v. *Major League Baseball Players Ass'n*, 95 F.3d 959 (10th Cir. 1996).

132. Eugene Volokh, "Freedom of Speech and the Right of Publicity," 40 HOUSTON L. Rev. 903, 924 (2003).

Conclusion: What Does the Future Hold?

133. H. Res. 210 (introduced April 12, 2005).

134. H.R. 683 (109th Congress).

135. 537 U.S. 418 (2003).

Books

Lessig. Lawrence. *Code and Other Laws of Cyberspace.* New York: Basic Books, 1999.

Lessig. Lawrence. *The Future of Ideas: The Fate of the Commons in a Connected World.* New York: Random House, 2001.

Litman, Jessica. *Digital Copyright.* Amherst, New York: Prometheus Books, 2001.

McCarthy, J. Thomas. *The Rights of Publicity and Privacy*, 2nd ed. Eagan, Minn.: Thomson West, 2005

Moser, David. *Music Copyright for the New Millenium.* Vallejo, California: ProMusic Press, 2002.

Samuels, Edward. *The Illustrated History of Copyright.* New York: Thomas Dunne Books, 2000.

Articles

Denneson, Travis J. "The Definitional Imbalance Between Copyright and the First Amendment." 30 WM. MITCHELL L. REV. 895 (2004).

Einhorn, Michael A. and Bill Rosenblatt. "Peer-to-Peer Networking and Digital Rights Management: How Market Tools Can Solve Copyright Problems." Cato Policy Analysis (2/17/05)

Engelman, Anna E. and Dale A. Scott, "Arrgh! Hollywood Targets Internet Piracy." 11 RICH. J.L. & TECH. 3 (2004).

Gilwit, Dara. "The Latest Cybersquatting Trend: Typosquatters, Their Changing Tactics, and How To Prevent Public Deception and Trademark Infringement." 11 WASH. U. J.L. & TECH. 267 (2003).

Ginsburg, Jane C. "How Copyright Got a Bad Name for Itself." 26 COLUM. J.L. & ARTS 61 (2002).

Greene, K.J. "Abusive Trademark Litigation and the Incredible Shrinking Confusion Doctrine—Trademark Abuse in the Context of Entertainment Media and Cyberspace," 27 HARV. J.L. & PUB. POL'Y 609 (2004).

Hudson, David. "Copyright and the First Amendment." First Amendment Center Online (8/05/01). Available online at *http://www.firstamendment-center.org/analysis.aspx?id=13828.*

Isenberg, Doug. "In Defense of Copyright Law." Gigalaw.com (Feb. 2003). Available online at *http://www.gigalaw.com/articles/2003-all/isenberg-2003-2-all.html.*

Kelley, Martha. "Is Liability Just a Link Away? Trademark Dilution By Tarnishment Under the Federal Trademark Dilution Act of 1995 and Hyperlinks on the World Wide Web." 9 J. INTELL. PROP. L. 361 (2002).

King, Howard. "Why Metallica Sued Napster." Findlaw.com (05/01/2000). Available online at *http://writ.news.findlaw.com/commentary/20000501_king.html.*

Koss, Natalie. "The Digital Music Dilemma: Protecting Copyright in the Age of Peer-to-Peer File Sharing." 5 VAND. J. ENT. L. & PRAC. 94 (2003).

Lutzker, Arnold P. & Susan J. "Altering the Contours of Copyright—The DMCA and the Unanswered Questions of Paramount Pictures Corp. v. 321 Studios." 21 SANTA CLARA COMPUTER & HIGH TECH. L.J. 561 (2005).

Madow, Michael. "Private Ownership of Public Image: Popular Culture and Publicity Rights." 81 CALIF. L. REV. 125 (1993).

Nimmer, Melvin. "The Right of Publicity." 19 LAW AND CONTEMPORARY PROBLEMS 203 (1954).

Prince, Daniel. "Cyber-Criticism and the Federal Trademark Dilution Act: Redefining the Noncommercial Use Exemption." 9 VA. J.L. & TECH. 12 (2004).

Sheets, Jason. "Copyright Misused: The Impact of the DMCA Anti-Circumvention Measures on Fair & Innovative Markets." 23 HASTINGS COMMENT L.J. 1 (2000).

Sorgen, Rebecca S. "Trademark Confronts Free Speech on the Information Superhighway: 'Cybergripers' Face a Constitutional Collision." 22 LOY. L.A. ENT. L. REV. 115 (2001).

Sprigman, Chris. "The Mouse that Ate the Public Domain: Disney, the Copyright Term Extension Act, and Eldred v. Ashcroft." Findlaw.com (3/5/02).

Travis, Hannibal. "The Battle for Mindshare: The Emerging Consensus that the First Amendment Protects Corporate Criticism and Parody on the Internet." 10 VA. J.L. & TECH. 3 (2005).

Volokh, Eugene. "Freedom of Speech and the Right of Publicity." 40 HOUS. L. REV. 903 (2003).

Webner, W. Mack and Leigh Ann Lindquist. "Transformation: The Bright Line Between Commercial Publicity Rights and the First Amendment." 37 AKRON L. REV. 171 (2004).

Websites

Findlaw

http://www.findlaw.com

Findlaw.com is perhaps the leading legal Website on the Internet. Findlaw has sections devoted to all aspects of intellectual property. Findlaw also has a commentary section that contains incisive and clear articles about a host of legal subjects, including intellectual property.

Recording Industry Association of America

http://www.riaa.org

The RIAA is the self-described "trade group that represents the U.S. recording industry." The RIAA works very hard to protect the intellectual property rights of musicians by combating piracy in the courts and in the court of public opinion.

Software and Information Industry Association

http://www.spa.org

Its Website states: "The Software & Information Industry Association is the principal trade association for the software and digital content industry." A section of its Website details the organization's anti-piracy efforts.

U.S. Copyright Office

http://www.copyright.gov

According to its Website, "the Copyright Office provides expert assistance to Congress on intellectual property matters; advises Congress on anticipated changes in U.S. copyright law; analyzes and assists in drafting copyright legislation and legislative reports and provides and undertakes studies for Congress." The site contains links to frequently asked questions, copyright laws, copyright basics and other information.

U.S. Patent and Trademark Office

http://www.uspto.gov

An agency of the Department of Commerce, the U.S. Patent and Trademark Office Website contains extensive information on trademark law and existing trademarks.

World Intellectual Property Organization

http://www.wipo.int

Its Website says that the "World Intellectual Property Organization (WIPO) is an international organization dedicated to promoting the use and protection of works of the human spirit." It has an incredible array of information on copyrights, trademarks and other forms of intellectual property law.

A & M Records, Inc. v. *Napster, Inc.*, 239 F.3d 1004 (9th Cir. 2001)

This is the famous Napster case. In this case, the 9th U.S. Circuit Court of Appeals determined that Napster was a contributory copyright infringer.

Bosley Medical Institute, Inc. v. *Kremer*, F.3d – (No. 04-55962)(9th Cir.) (4/5/05).

Trademark and cybersquatting case.

Campbell v. *Acuff-Rose Music, Inc.*, 510 U.S. 569 (1994).

U.S. Supreme Court decision on parody and fair use.

Carson v. *Here's Johnny Portable Toilets*, 698 F.2d 831 (6th Cir. 1983).

In this case, the 6th U.S. Circuit Court of Appeals determined that a Michigan company that used famed entertainer's famous trademark slogan "Here's Johnny" violated the publicity rights of the entertainer. It contains a good discussion of the right of publicity.

Comedy III Productions, Inc. v. *Saderup, Inc.*, 25 Cal. 4th 387 (2001).

The California Supreme Court ruled that an artist who made T-shirts with the pictures of the Three Stooges violated the intellectual property rights of the Stooges' heirs.

Doe v. *TCI Cablevision*, 110 S.W.3d 363 (Mo. 2003).

In this right of publicity case, the Missouri Supreme Court ruled that a comic book creator and publisher were liable for using the name of a former hockey player as an evil character in the comic book series. The court determined that the hockey player's publicity rights were infringed upon. It is considered a very controversial ruling.

Eldred v. *Ashcroft*, 537 U.S. 186 (2003).

The U.S. Supreme Court ruled 7–2 that the Copyright Term Extension Act is constitutional. The majority rejected a challenge to the law on copyright clause and First Amendment grounds. The Copyright Term Extension Act extended the term of copyright by 20 additional years.

Haelen Laboratories, Inc. v. *Topps Chewing Gum, Inc.*, 202 F.2d 866 (2nd Cir. 1953).

This is the decision in which Judge Jerome Frank first coined the term "right of publicity" to discuss the intellectual property rights that persons have in the value of their name for commercial purposes. It is considered the beginning of the right of publicity action.

Harper & Row v. *Nation Enterprises*, 471 U.S. 539 (1985).

This is an important U.S. Supreme Court case discussing the contours of the fair use exception in copyright law. The Court ruled that the *Nation* magazine committed copyright infringement and was not entitled to fair use when it published excerpts of the as-yet unpublished memoirs of President Gerald Ford.

Hoffman v. *Capital Cities*, 255 F.3d 1180 (9th Cir. 2001).

In this decision, the 9th Circuit reversed a jury verdict for famous actor Dustin Hoffman, who alleged his intellectual property rights were violated when a magazine ran a digitally altered photograph of Hoffman in his movie *Tootsie*.

In Re: Aimster Copyright Litigation, 334 F.3d 643 (7th Cir. 2003).

In this music piracy/contributory infringement case, the 7th U.S. Circuit Court of Appeals held that Aimster, unlike Napster, was liable for copyright infringement because it engaged in "willful blindness" as to the direct infringing activities of its customers. The decision was authored by Judge Richard Posner, one of the most influential appellate court judges.

Lucent Technologies, Inc. v. *Lucentsucks.com*, 95 F.Supp. 2d 528, 536 (E.D. Va. 2000).

This is one of the very first cybersquatting cases involving a cybergriper site. Although it was decided on jurisdictional grounds, the judge indicated that a site devoted to consumer commentary and criticism would not be subject to the trademark laws.

Morrison & Foerster LLP v. *Wick*, 94 F.Supp. 2d 1125 (D. Co. 2000).

In this cybersquatting case, a federal district court ruled in favor of a law firm who was battling an individual who had bought up several domain names containing the law firm's names. It is one of the first published decisions involving the Anti-Cybersquatting Consumer Protection Act of 1999.

Moseley v. *V Secret Catalogue, Inc.*, 537 U.S. 418 (2003).

This is the first decision by the U.S. Supreme Court dealing with the Federal Trademark Dilution Act. The Supreme Court ruled that a plaintiff alleging trademark dilution must show some actual proof of dilution. Congress is considering legislation that would overrule this decision.

Parks v. *LaFace Records*, 329 F.3d 437 (6th Cir. 2003).

The 6th U.S. Circuit Court of Appeals ruled that Rosa Parks can sue the group OutKast for trademark infringement and right of publicity because the group did not ask permission to use Parks' name in one of their songs. The court believed that the group used Parks' name for commercial purposes to draw attention to its song.

Sony Corporation of America v. *Universal City Studios, Inc.*, 464 U.S. 417 (1984).

In this decision, the U.S. Supreme Court ruled that Sony was not liable for contributory copyright infringement for its VCR product. The court ruled that the VCR was capable of substantial, noninfringing uses. The *Sony* case is the leading precedent that the Supreme Court is evaluating in the current music privacy case, *Metro-Goldwyn-Mayer* v. *Grokster*.

Universal City Studios, Inc. v. *Corley*, 273 F.3d 429 (2nd Cir. 2001).

In this case, the 2nd U.S. Circuit Court of Appeals rejected constitutional challenges to the Digital Millennium Copyright Act, which contains provisions prohibiting the circumvention of digital copyright protection schemes. The appeals court determined that there was no fair use exception to the anti-circumvention provision.

Zacchini v. *Scripps-Howard Broadcasting Co.*, 433 U.S. 562 (1977).

This is the first and only U.S. Supreme Court decision on the right of publicity. The Court ruled 5–4 that a news station violated the publicity rights of an entertainer when the station ran the entire 15-second act of the performer on the news without compensating the entertainer any money.

Terms and Concepts

contributory copyright infringement
copyright
copyright clause
Copyright Management System
cybersquatting
Digital Millenium Copyright Act
dilution
fair use
First Amendment
inducement
infringement
Lanham Act
noncommercial speech
patent
publicity
trademark
transformative

Beginning Legal Research

The goal of POINT/COUNTERPOINT is not only to provide the reader with an introduction to a controversial issue affecting society, but also to encourage the reader to explore the issue more fully. This appendix, then, is meant to serve as a guide to the reader in researching the current state of the law as well as exploring some of the public-policy arguments as to why existing laws should be changed or new laws are needed.

Like many types of research, legal research has become much faster and more accessible with the invention of the Internet. This appendix discusses some of the best starting points, but of course "surfing the Net" will uncover endless additional sources of information—some more reliable than others. Some important sources of law are not yet available on the Internet, but these can generally be found at the larger public and university libraries. Librarians usually are happy to point patrons in the right direction.

The most important source of law in the United States is the Constitution. Originally enacted in 1787, the Constitution outlines the structure of our federal government and sets limits on the types of laws that the federal government and state governments can pass. Through the centuries, a number of amendments have been added to or changed in the Constitution, most notably the first ten amendments, known collectively as the Bill of Rights, which guarantee important civil liberties. Each state also has its own constitution, many of which are similar to the U.S. Constitution. It is important to be familiar with the U.S. Constitution because so many of our laws are affected by its requirements. State constitutions often provide protections of individual rights that are even stronger than those set forth in the U.S. Constitution.

Within the guidelines of the U.S. Constitution, Congress—both the House of Representatives and the Senate—passes bills that are either vetoed or signed into law by the President. After the passage of the law, it becomes part of the United States Code, which is the official compilation of federal laws. The state legislatures use a similar process, in which bills become law when signed by the state's governor. Each state has its own official set of laws, some of which are published by the state and some of which are published by commercial publishers. The U.S. Code and the state codes are an important source of legal research; generally, legislators make efforts to make the language of the law as clear as possible.

However, reading the text of a federal or state law generally provides only part of the picture. In the American system of government, after the legislature passes laws and the executive (U.S. President or state governor) signs them, it is up to the judicial branch of the government, the court system, to interpret the laws and decide whether they violate any provision of the Constitution. At the state level, each state's supreme court has the ultimate authority in determining what a law means and whether or not it violates the state constitution. However, the federal courts—headed by the U.S. Supreme Court—can review state laws and court decisions to determine whether they violate federal laws or the U.S. Constitution. For example, a state court may find that a particular criminal law is valid under the state's constitution, but a federal court may then review the state court's decision and determine that the law is invalid under the U.S. Constitution.

It is important, then, to read court decisions when doing legal research. The Constitution uses language that is intentionally very general—for example, prohibiting "unreasonable searches and seizures" by the police—and court cases often provide more guidance. For example, the U.S. Supreme Court's 2001 decision in *Kyllo* v. *United States* held that scanning the outside of a person's house using a heat sensor to determine whether the person is growing marijuana is unreasonable—*if* it is done without a search warrant secured from a judge. Supreme Court decisions provide the most definitive explanation of the law of the land, and it is therefore important to include these in research. Often, when the Supreme Court has not decided a case on a particular issue, a decision by a federal appeals court or a state supreme court can provide guidance; but just as laws and constitutions can vary from state to state, so can federal courts be split on a particular interpretation of federal law or the U.S. Constitution. For example, federal appeals courts in Louisiana and California may reach opposite conclusions in similar cases.

Lawyers and courts refer to statutes and court decisions through a formal system of citations. Use of these citations reveals which court made the decision (or which legislature passed the statute) and when and enables the reader to locate the statute or court case quickly in a law library. For example, the legendary Supreme Court case *Brown* v. *Board of Education* has the legal citation 347 U.S. 483 (1954). At a law library, this 1954 decision can be found on page 483 of volume 347 of the U.S. Reports, the official collection of the Supreme Court's decisions. Citations can also be helpful in locating court cases on the Internet.

Understanding the current state of the law leads only to a partial under-standing of the issues covered by the POINT/COUNTERPOINT series. For a fuller understanding of the issues, it is necessary to look at public-policy arguments that the current state of the law is not adequately addressing the issue. Many groups lobby for new legislation or changes to existing legislation; the National Rifle Association (NRA), for example, lobbies Congress and the state legislatures constantly to make existing gun control laws less restrictive and not to pass additional laws. The NRA and other groups dedicated to various causes might also intervene in pending court cases: a group such as Planned Parenthood might file a brief *amicus curiae* (as "a friend of the court")—called an "amicus brief"—in a lawsuit that could affect abortion rights. Interest groups also use the media to influence public opinion, issuing press releases and frequently appearing in interviews on news programs and talk shows. The books in POINT/COUNTERPOINT list some of the interest groups that are active in the issue at hand, but in each case there are countless other groups working at the local, state, and national levels. It is important to read everything with a critical eye, for sometimes interest groups present information in a way that can be read only to their advantage. The informed reader must always look for bias.

Finding sources of legal information on the Internet is relatively simple thanks to "portal" sites such as FindLaw (*www.findlaw.com*), which provides access to a variety of constitutions, statutes, court opinions, law review articles, news articles, and other resources—including all Supreme Court decisions issued since 1893. Other useful sources of information include the U.S. Government Printing Office (*www.gpo.gov*), which contains a complete copy of the U.S. Code, and the Library of Congress's THOMAS system (*thomas.loc.gov*), which offers access to bills pending before Congress as well as recently passed laws. Of course, the Internet changes every second of every day, so it is best to do some independent searching. Most cases, studies, and opinions that are cited or referred to in public debate can be found online— and *everything* can be found in one library or another.

The Internet can provide a basic understanding of most important legal issues, but not all sources can be found there. To find some documents it is necessary to visit the law library of a university or a public law library; some cities have public law libraries, and many library systems keep legal documents at the main branch. On the following page are some common citation forms.

COMMON CITATION FORMS

Source of Law	Sample Citation	Notes
U.S. Supreme Court	*Employment Division v. Smith*, 485 U.S. 660 (1988)	The U.S. Reports is the official record of Supreme Court decisions. There is also an unofficial Supreme Court ("S. Ct.") reporter.
U.S. Court of Appeals	*United States v. Lambert*, 695 F.2d 536 (11th Cir.1983)	Appellate cases appear in the Federal Reporter, designated by "F." The 11th Circuit has jurisdiction in Alabama, Florida, and Georgia.
U.S. District Court	*Carillon Importers, Ltd. v. Frank Pesce Group, Inc.*, 913 F.Supp. 1559 (S.D.Fla.1996)	Federal trial-level decisions are reported in the Federal Supplement ("F. Supp."). Some states have multiple federal districts; this case originated in the Southern District of Florida.
U.S. Code	Thomas Jefferson Commemoration Commission Act, 36 U.S.C., §149 (2002)	Sometimes the popular names of legislation—names with which the public may be familiar—are included with the U.S. Code citation.
State Supreme Court	*Sterling v. Cupp*, 290 Ore. 611, 614, 625 P.2d 123, 126 (1981)	The Oregon Supreme Court decision is reported in both the state's reporter and the Pacific regional reporter.
State Statute	Pennsylvania Abortion Control Act of 1982, 18 Pa. Cons. Stat. 3203-3220 (1990)	States use many different citation formats for their statutes.

115

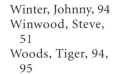

page:

20: Associated Press Graphics
31: Associated Press, AP/Chris Pizzello
41: Associated Press, AP/
George Nikitin
53: Associated Press, AP/
Gerald Herbert

60: Associated Press Graphics
79: Associated Press, AP/
Douglas C. Pizac
95: Associated Press, AP/
Lm Otero

Cover: © Steve Marcus/Las Vegas Sun/Reuters/CORBIS

DAVID L. HUDSON, JR., is an author-attorney who has published widely on First Amendment and other constitutional law issues. Hudson is a research attorney with the First Amendment Center at Vanderbilt and a First Amendment contributing editor to the American Bar Association's *Preview of the United States Supreme Court Cases.* He obtained his undergraduate degree from Duke University and his law degree from Vanderbilt University Law School.

ALAN MARZILLI, M.A., J.D., of Durham, North Carolina, is an independent consultant working on several ongoing projects for state and federal government agencies and nonprofit organizations. He has spoken about mental health issues in thirty states, the District of Columbia, and Puerto Rico; his work includes training mental health administrators, nonprofit management and staff, and people with mental illness and their family members on a wide variety of topics, including effective advocacy, community-based mental health services, and housing. He has written several hand-books and training curricula that are used nationally. He managed statewide and national mental health advocacy programs and worked for several public interest lobbying organizations in Washington, D.C., while studying law at Georgetown University.